Palgrave CIBFR Studies in Islamic Finance

Series editors
Nafis Alam
Business School
Sunway University
Selangor, Malaysia

Syed Aun R. Rizvi
Suleman Dawood School of Business
Lahore University of Management Sciences
Lahore, Pakistan

The Centre for Islamic Business and Finance Research (CIBFR) is a global center of excellence for developing Islamic business and finance as a scientific academic discipline and for promoting Islamic financial products, monetary and fiscal policies, and business and trade practices. Based at The University of Nottingham campus in Malaysia, CIBFR looks at the multi-dimensional aspects of Islamic business, cutting across the major themes of Islamic economics, Islamic finance and the Halal market. True to the pioneering nature of the research CIBFR undertakes, the Palgrave CIBFR Series in Islamic Finance offers empirical enquiries into key issues and challenges in modern Islamic finance. It explores issues in such varied fields as Islamic accounting, Takaful (Islamic insurance), Islamic financial services marketing, and ethical and socially responsible investing.

More information about this series at
http://www.springer.com/series/15190

Syed Aun R. Rizvi · Irum Saba
Editors

Developments in Islamic Finance

Challenges and Initiatives

palgrave
macmillan

Editors
Syed Aun R. Rizvi
Suleman Dawood School of Business
Lahore University of Management Sciences
(LUMS)
Lahore, Pakistan

Irum Saba
Institute of Business Administration
Karachi, Pakistan

Palgrave CIBFR Studies in Islamic Finance
ISBN 978-3-319-59341-8 ISBN 978-3-319-59342-5 (eBook)
DOI 10.1007/978-3-319-59342-5

Library of Congress Control Number: 2017944223

Cover illustration: Pattern adapted from an Indian cotton print produced in the 19th century

Printed on acid-free paper

This Palgrave Macmillan imprint is published by Springer Nature
The registered company is Springer International Publishing AG
The registered company address is: Gewerbestrasse 11, 6330 Cham, Switzerland

Preface

This book has been born out of the need to further the development in Islamic finance. The critique of Islamic finance as limited to a segment of society following a specific faith has developed over the years. With the growth in the financial sector globally, Islamic finance has shown tremendous potential in terms of both growth and resilience.

This book brings to forth new ideas and innovative solutions within the paradigm of Islamic finance which the world faces today. The first chapter apprises the readers of the status of Islamic finance, bringing in facts and figures and highlighting the pitfalls of the recent growth in Islamic finance.

The fastest-growing sector of the Islamic finance is the fixed-income instrument of Sukuk. With our world facing a challenge of water deprivation, and concerns being raised over what we would leave behind in terms of the water supply for our future generations to come, this book introduces an innovative Sukuk instrument which addresses some of the concerns in terms of financing of water-based projects. With taking Malaysia as a case study, second chapter argues for the benefits of reducing non-revenue water (NRW) in terms of value and solving the issue through structuring green sukuk to finance NRW work. With the focus and development of Sukuk structures and innovative instruments, the concern of financial mismanagement and defaults has become a reality. This book also highlights these challenges by taking the case of Villamar Sukuk in trying to decode the nature and causes of the difficulties encountered in quick settlement of defaulted sukuk.

Sukuks are not the only sector raising interest for innovation and further inquiry. A thought-provoking proposal is put forward in this book which introduces a concept of saving-based Takaful products that can help people in Pakistan in planning the future for their children's education. With the global focus on providing quality education to our kids, this case study provides some empirical findings which aim to further encourage thought and development in the educational sector.

While instrument-specific debates engage readers and practitioners across the breadth of this book, taking a break from the tradition, and keeping in mind the global nature of the world we live in, a case plan on introducing Islamic finance to unchartered territories is presented by the author/s through building a case for Islamic finance beyond its faith-based association only.

While no discussion is complete without a macroeconomic aspect, this book concludes with an insightful article on explaining the role of Islamic finance in a multipolar world and the emergence of Black Swan events. A strong argument is built on the role of Islamic finance by arguing that continuation of debt-based financing regime will not necessarily allow the benefits of emerging multipolarity to accrue to the world economy. The new system can be more effective with a new regime of financing. Indications are that almost all emerging countries in Asia are actively considering risk sharing via Islamic finance as a possible alternative.

Lahore, Pakistan Syed Aun R. Rizvi

Contents

Notes on Contributors

Dr. Baharom Abdul Hamid is currently the Associate Professor of Economics at INCEIF. He is also the Director of Research at the university. His areas of interest are applied econometrics and economics. He can be contacted at baharom@inceif.org.

Dr. Farrukh Habib is a Research Fellow at the International Shariah Research Academy (ISRA). He holds a Ph.D. in Islamic Finance from INCEIF and can be contacted at farrukh@isra.my.

Dr. Muhammad Imran is associated with Institute of Business Administration, Karachi, Pakistan.

Dr. Salman Syed Ali is associated with Islamic Research Training Institute (IRTI) at IDB. He has extensively published on Islamic Capital Markets and can be contacted at ssyedali@isdb.org.

Dr. Wajahat Azmi is a Post-Doctoral Research Fellow at INCEIF. He holds a Ph.D. in Islamic finance previously and specialized in ethical and Islamic funds. He can be contacted at wajahat_azmi@yahoo.com

Dr. Irum Saba is an ex-banking regulator turned researcher. She is an Assistant Professor at the Institute of Business Administration in Karachi. She can be contacted at isaba@iba.edu.pk.

Kulsanofer Syed Thajudeen is a doctorol candidate at INCEIF. She can be contacted at kulsanofer@gmail.com

Mohsin Ali is an ex-banker turned researcher. He is currently pursuing his Ph.D. in Islamic finance at INCEIF. His area of interest is Islamic banking and financial inclusion. He can be contacted at Mohsin.ali121@gmail.com.

Mohsin Khawja is associated with Center of Research Excellence for Islamic Banking & Finance, Research Institute, King Fahd University of Petroleum and Minerals, Dhahran, Kingdom of Saudi Arabia.

Mughees Shaukat is Head of Islamic Finance, College of Banking and Financial Studies, under Central Bank of Oman, Muscat, Oman. He can be contacted at mughees@cbfs.edu.om.

Professor Dr. Abbas Mirakhor is the former Executive Dean, IMF, USA, and the first holder of the chair in Islamic finance at INCEIF, Kuala Lumpur, Malaysia. He can be contacted at abbasmirakhor@inceif.org.

Zaheer Anwer is an ex-banker turned researcher. He is currently pursuing his Ph.D. in Islamic finance at INCEIF. His area of interest is Islamic banking and financial inclusion. He can be contacted at Mohsin.ali121@gmail.com

List of Figures

Islamic Finance—Local and Global Status

Sukuk for the Financing of Non-revenue Water Management: Malaysia as a Case Study

Introducing Islamic Finance in Unchartered Economies: The Case of Canada

List of Tables

Towards a Robust *Shariah* Screening Criterion for Stocks

Islamic Finance, in the Age of Black Swans and Complexities, for a Multipolar World

Islamic Finance—Local and Global Status

Irum Saba

Abstract This article apprises the readers on the current status of Islamic finance across the world. Islamic finance though nascent has grown manifolds in the recent years and has spread across many different jurisdictions. With Pakistan as a Muslim-majority nation, it has been at forefront of the efforts and growth of Islamic finance. The article provides some insights into way forward for the industry.

Keywords Islamic banking · Islamic finance · Shariah · Islamic windows · Islamic Financial Services Board (IFSB)

1 Introduction

One of the biggest challenges faced by the world is to have a balanced and successful economic system without any financial crisis. Muslims of the twentieth century worldwide have been trying to establish

I. Saba (✉)
Institute of Business Administration (IBA), Karachi, Pakistan
e-mail: isaba@iba.edu.pk

S.A.R. Rizvi and I. Saba (eds.), *Developments in Islamic Finance*, Palgrave CIBFR Studies in Islamic Finance, DOI 10.1007/978-3-319-59342-5_1

a financial system and financial institutions in accordance with the principles of Shariah, or Islamic law. In an environment where usually the entire financial system, from the sovereign government to financial markets and small- and large-scale financial institutions (FIs), is inherently based on interest, this is indeed a formidable task.

The term "Islamic finance" is often heard of as an oxymoron. The listener thinks of Islam as a philosophy that guides one to prepare for the life of the hereafter and implies purification from greed and perhaps even a general disinterest in the pursuit of wealth, prosperity, or economic gain. Finance and banking, on the other hand, is to a great extent about maximizing shareholder's wealth, depositors' savings, investors' returns, corporate culture, and surviving in the extremely competitive market. Then, how can a system or organization pertaining to financial industry be Islamic? One way to analyze this question is to think about "Islamic" finance as simply "Islamic law-compliant" finance—a system which tries to embody the economic and social teachings of Islam.

It is sometimes perceived that a religious system of law traditionally focuses only on matters pertaining to worship. It may even be conventional, old-fashioned, limited in its use, or at least difficult in widely applying it in the complex and dynamic matters of an economy. So how can it provide precise, practicable rulings and principles for financial systems? The fact is that Islamic Law, or Shariah, prerogatives to be a "complete code of life," and though there are elements of flexibility, custom, *Masalaha al Mursalaha* (public benefit), and valid differences of opinion in its legal system, it claims to be an applicable system for all societies and all times to come. Islamic Law, or the Shariah (meaning a "path" to righteousness), can be subdivided into two broad categories: Fiqh-ul-Ibaadat (laws pertaining to worship matters) and Fiqh-ul-Muamalat (laws pertaining to human dealings). The latter is of special relevance to Islamic finance, and it includes Islamic law for valid contracts, valid sales, halal (permissible), Makrooh (disliked) and haram (impermissible) activities or sources of income, laws relating to inheritance, marriage and divorce, relationships, transactions, governments and economics, wealth management, modesty and interpersonal interactions, etc. While this is a very broad category, Fiqh-ul-Ibaadat, on the other hand, deals almost exclusively with matters of worship and a Muslim's personal purification and relationship with his/her Creator. It includes rules for Salah, fasting, pilgrimage (Hajj and Umrah), prayers and invocations, and purification from diseases of the heart such as greed, jealousy, pride, anger, and lust Interestingly, the sources of these two categories of Islamic law and their methodologies are the same. There are, of course, some important matters that fall in an overlap—Zakat, for instance, is a mandatory charity on all able Muslims and one of the five main acts of worship, covered in Fiqh-ul-Ibadat, but its rules are much relevant to the economy and Islamic financial systems as well.

Islamic banking is simply a subset of Islamic finance: an industry that includes banks, central banks, development banks, financial markets, Takaful (insurance) companies, asset management companies, brokerage houses, research and educational centers, and Islamic capital markets. The main objective of Islamic finance is to enable a financial system that is stable; fulfills the *halal* (permissible) economic needs of the consumers, corporations, and government in the economy; supports the real economy; and leads to an equitable distribution and circulation of wealth in the society, while avoiding impermissible activities, trades, and transactions. The main impermissible transaction elements according to the Islamic Law (Shariah) include Riba (interest), Maisir (gambling), Gharar (excessive uncertainty), and Uqood-ul-Fasida (or invalid transactions, such as forward sale, short selling, sale of debt, and sale and buy back). A financial institution or a firm that is compliant with Islamic law is also forbidden from dealing in any *Haram* (impressible in Shariah) activities or industries, such as alcohol, pork, tobacco, and Haram entertainment. Hence, an Islamic financial institution (IFI), or a "Shariah-compliant" bank, is simply an institute that meets the economic or financial demands of its consumers in a way that does not go against the commands of the Shariah.

An Islamic economic system, at least theoretically, strives to achieve some greater principal objectives of the Islamic Law with its activities, modes, rules, and prohibitions. According to the reputed historic Islamic scholar, Imam Al Ghazali, the ultimate objectives of Islamic Law, or the *Maqasid al Shariah* (the main Objectives of the Islamic Law), can be briefly described as:

> The very objective of the Shariah is to promote the well-being of the people, which lies in safeguarding their faith (din), their lives (nafs), their intellect (aql), their posterity (nasl), and their wealth (mal). Whatever ensures the safeguarding of these five serves the public interest and is desirable, and whatever hurts them is against public interest and its removal is desirable.[1]

He lists five elements that Islam attempts to protect: (1) Religion, (2) Lives, (3) Intellect, (4) Lineage, and (5) Property, wealth, or economic prosperity. Shariah is based on the four main sources of Islamic Law: the *Quran*, the *Sunnah* (which includes the sayings, practices, and tacit approvals of the Prophet Muhammad (Peace be upon him)), *Ijma* (consensus of the Islamic jurists/scholars on a matter), and *Qiyas* (analogical deductions, or juristic efforts/Ijtihad of qualified Islamic scholars on a legal matter not explicitly answered in Quran, Sunnah, or Ijma). As Islam is a religion that claims to be a complete code of life, the Shariah offers its followers commands, prohibitions, and guidelines on beliefs (Aqaa'id, e.g., in One God, revealed in books, prophets, angels, Life after death, etc.), Worship matters (Ibaadat, such as fasting, prayers, Zakat, pilgrimage), and human-to-human dealings (or Muamalat). The latter includes matters relating to transactions and economics and finance.

Though Islamic financial institutions are forbidden legally from undertaking any transactions that involve Riba or any of the other Shariah-prohibited elements, nevertheless, they can use certain modes of financing that are prescribed by Islam. These can be summarized into profit-sharing modes, leasing modes, and structures based on sale of assets (usually for a profit). Shariah compliant modes used in Islamic finance worldwide help the financial institutions in generating income, investing, or managing their liquidity including the following:

One of the most common modes of financing used by Islamic financial institutions (IFIs) is *Murabaha*. This is a kind of sale where the IFI sells a customer (firm or individual) a specific kind of asset they require (such as a vehicle, machinery, and commodity), that is in its possession. As this is a sale and not an interest-based loan, the price of the asset is the sum of the original price (which is disclosed to the client) and an agreed profit margin. Hence, Murabaha is also called "mark-up sale."

Usually, Murabaha practiced is a credit sale (Bai Muajjal), where the client agrees to pay the price deferred, as installments or as one lump sum payments. Murabaha is used only for short-term financing in some countries and for both short-term and long-term project financing in others. It is very common in consumer financing and for meeting the financing needs of the exports/importers.

One common use of Murabaha in the global industry is the *Commodity Murabaha*. Here, the IFI purchases a commodity, such as oil and rice, from a seller/broker and then sells it to the customer (firm that needs it).

While Murabaha is essentially a debt-based mode of financing, IFIs also use profit-sharing contracts to generate their income. One common mode is the *Mudarabah*—a partnership contract between a capital provider (called Rab-ul-Maal) and an entrepreneur (called Mudarib). The Rab-ul-Maal (who can be more than one) is the sole contributor of the capital, and the Mudarib alone manages the funds/business. The underlying business is Shariah compliant, and a profit-sharing ratio (PSR) is pre-agreed between both partners. Any profits arising from the activities are hence shared between them. As per the rules of the Shariah, any loss arising (not attributed to the negligence of the Mudarib) is borne solely by the Rab-ul-Maal (as losses have to be shared in the ratio of capital contribution). Many Islamic scholars have termed the partnership between the Prophet (pbuh) himself and Hazrat Khadija (RA) as a Mudarabah, where the former undertook trade caravans from Makkah to Syria from the capital provided by the latter. Today, many of the deposits of Islamic banks are based on underlying Mudarabah contracts in several South Asian and GCC countries. The central banks issue detailed regulations on the profit and loss sharing of deposit pools. In the modern Islamic capital markets industry, Syndicate Mudarabah is also used—where two or more investors contribute their funds for a project run by the management/investment company.

Another similar profit-sharing partnership is the *Musharakah*. Here, all partners of the business agree to share profits arising from a halal (permissible) enterprise according to a pre-agreed ratio. Unlike Mudarabah, however, there is no one partner who is the sole contributor of capital or the sole manager of the enterprise. In principle, all partners can share in the management of the firm. Any losses arising have to be shared in the ratio of the partners' capital contributions. Musharakah is used for project financing by IFIs in several countries. Syndicate Musharakah is also possible, where the partners share in the ownership of a property, equipment, etc. and share profits according to the PSR. Musharakah and Mudarabah are also used in the underlying Sukuk structures and give the Islamic finance industry risk-sharing modes of financing.

An *Ijarah* is a lease contract, where the usufruct of a specified asset is leased to a customer for an agreed period against specified rentals. It is sometimes accompanied by a unilateral promise from one of the contracting parties to gift (Hiba) the asset after all rentals are received, or to sell it at a given price to the other party.

Ijarah is a very common mode of financing used in retail as well as investment banking. It is used extensively by Islamic banks in car and house financing and is also used for financing premises, plants, machinery, etc. for firms. In fact, in the Islamic capital markets industry, many of the modern-day Sukuk issues are based on the underlying Ijarah contracts.

Other sale-based modes used by IFIs globally include *Salam* and *Istisna*. Although generally forward and future sales are not permitted under the Shariah, Salam and Istisna are two exceptions. In Salam, a seller sells a specified commodity, such as rice, sugar, and wheat, whose type, quantity, specifications, and price are known and agreed. The full price is paid by the buyer on spot, while the commodity's delivery is deferred to a fixed future date. Istisna, on the other hand, is the sale of a specified asset, such as machinery, power plant, and house, that is to be manufactured/constructed by the seller as per the specified demands of the client. The seller/manufacturer signs an obligation to use their own materials to deliver the asset to the buyer for the agreed price, at a future date (not necessarily fixed as in Salam). The price can be paid on spot, in a lump sum, or installments. Salam is frequently used by IFIs to finance the agricultural sector, whereas Istisna-based financing contracts are used for project financing for various industries, such as in the energy sector and infrastructure.

Additionally, Islamic finance industry creates hybrid structures to fulfill the economic or financing needs of its customers. One such popular structure is that of *Diminishing Musharakah*, a sort of a mixture of Ijarah and Musharakah. In this, two partners, such as a customer and an Islamic bank, jointly purchase an asset that the customer needs and agree that, over a period of time, one partner (the bank) will gradually purchase the equity shares of the other partner, until the customer is the sole owner of the asset. The rentals are adjusted according to the share of ownership of the partners. For example, financier A and customer B jointly buy a plant costing $10 million, with A supplying 80% and B 20% of the capital, and the agreed rental is $10,000 per quarter. B then signs a separate promise with A to buy one of A's eight ownership shares every quarter (for its price of $1 million). Hence, after the first quarter, B owns 30% of the asset, while A owns only 70%. Hence, the rentals payable are decreased from $8000 to $7000. Two years later, when B has bought all eight of A's shares, B becomes the sole owner of the plant, and the rentals cease. Diminishing Musharakah is much commonly used not only in consumer financing (usually for homes), but also for long-term project financing and as an underlying contract in certain Sukuk issues.

IFIs can also earn halal income using agency structures. *Wakala* is an agency contract where the client (principal) appoints an institution as an agent (Wakeel) to carry out some business or management on their behalf. The Wakeel is usually entitled to a fee as remuneration for his services. Modern-day IFIs operate mutual funds, income and equity funds, etc. based on Wakala contracts. Wakala is also used as a supporting contract in many diversified Islamic finance products, such as Ijarah or Murabaha (which often includes a client buying a specific asset as an agent on the IFI's behalf), or Takaful, where the Takaful operator manages the pool of funds as a Wakeel and earns a fee.

An Islamic financial system also has some inherent structures that can contribute to fulfilling the Maqasid ul Shariah highlighted above.

One very important concept in the Islamic finance landscape, particularly the Islamic capital markets industry, is that of Sukuk. *Sukuk structures* are certificates of ownership that are Shariah compliant. While we know that financial institutions need tradable instruments such as bonds and swaps for investing and liquidity management purposes, the Shariah compliance aspect of these instruments poses a significant problem: Firstly, bonds and swaps would not be permissible for IFIs due to the fact that they include Riba. The reader would recall that, apart from the interest coupon payments of bonds, money is classified as one of the "homogenous" commodities (such as gold and silver) on which rules of Riba-al Fadl apply and which cannot be traded in unequal amounts (excluding a process such as profit sharing, sale, and lease) without incurring Riba. Secondly, even without the interest component, and even if the certificates were (hypothetically) being traded at par, bonds and loans are classical debt instruments, and the Shariah forbids the sale of debt (*Bai ud Dain*) to third parties. This means that trading these instruments in secondary markets is also not permissible for IFIs.

Sukuk solve these problems by being structured as certificates that represent a proportional undivided ownership share in real, tangible assets. These assets are usually for a specific project or for an investment activity that is Shariah compliant.

To illustrate this with an example, suppose the Company X needs to raise $30 million for the construction of an apartment complex. It calculates that the quarterly rental payable on the property is $900,000. It approaches an IFI which structures a Shariah compliant Sukuk for this project, based on the Ijarah. The $30 million complex is divided into 30,000 certificates, each worth $1000 and representing 1/30,000 of the ownership of the asset. After 2 years, once the rentals start, each certificate holder is entitled to receive $30 payment (or 3%). Since these certificates represent ownership in the underlying asset, they can also be traded in the open market and hence provide liquidity management options to IFIs. Sukuk are issued by firms as well as governments (sovereign Sukuk), are usually rated by credit rating agencies to reflect their risks, and can be both debt based and equity based. Apart from Ijarah, they can be structured on different structures, such as Musharakah, Mudarabah, Diminishing Musharakah, Wakala, Istisna, or Salam.

Sukuk represent a very important part of the global Islamic capital markets industry. The issuance of international Sukuk commenced in 2001, and from 2001 to 2014, the cumulative value of total issuance reached to US$91.77 billion (with some decline in 2009 and 2010). Combined with this growth in value, the variety in Sukuk structures also increased, starting from Ijarah-based Sukuk to those including

Musharakah (profit and loss sharing). Corporate and sovereign Sukuk have been issued in many countries, including Malaysia, Bahrain, Kuwait, Qatar, Jordan, Saudi Arabia, UAE, and most recently, even UK, USA, and Pakistan.

Central banks play a key role in developing their country's Islamic capital markets, by developing legal frameworks for Sukuk issues. For instance, the government of Bahrain issued Salam Sukuk as an alternative to Treasury bills for its IFIs and Ijarah Sukuk as an alternative to bonds. Similarly, the governments of Malaysia, Jordan, and Qatar also issued sovereign Sukuk. Britain famously became the first Western government to issue sovereign Sukuk in June 2014, with a £200 million Ijarah Sukuk issue, at a profit rate of 2.036% and a 5-year tenure, which was not issued at any premium (less profit rate as compared to conventional bonds) and was famously oversubscribed almost 12 times due to the high demand (with orders totaling £2.3 billion).

2 The Current Global Status of the Islamic Finance Industry

Globally, the Islamic finance industry has a total size of US$1.88 trillion by the end of 2015 (IFSB report 2016) and is estimated to reach $3.2 trillion (or $6 trillion by some estimates) according to ICD Thomson Reuters Islamic Finance Development Indicator. However, the year 2015 saw a relatively modest growth in the Islamic finance industry, noticeably lower than the double-digit growth rates of previous years. This was attributed (IFSB Stability Report 2016) to low energy prices and economic growth rates, some geopolitical conflicts, and in particular, the exchange rate depreciations in many key Islamic finance markets, including Turkey, Malaysia, and Indonesia. Given the withdrawal of a major Sukuk issuer from the global market, and downward pressures in the international equity markets, the size of outstanding global Sukuk declined by 1.4% to US$290.6 billion, from US$294.7 billion (Financial Services Report 2015). Islamic funds' assets also observed a decline by 8.4%, although the Islamic banking sector, by far the dominating segment in the international Islamic finance industry, observed a modest growth of 1.4%. The global Takaful sector was estimated at US$23.2 billion in 2015. Though the whole industry is still only about 1% of the global finance industry and largely segregated in some jurisdictions, there is no doubt that it has witnessed consistent, profound growth in the past 30 years.

Compared to the conventional industry, the global Islamic finance industry, which includes Islamic banking (dominant), Islamic capital markets, and Takaful (Islamic insurance), has witnessed a far more aggressive growth. According to the March 2016 Islamic Finance Bulletin,[2] between 2011 and 2015, the Islamic finance industry grew at a compound annual growth rate of 3.6%, compared to only 1.5% of the conventional industry. However, the industry is only about 1% of the size of the global financial industry today (Fig. 1).

In terms of jurisdictions, Islamic finance is present in almost 90 countries across the globe, with about 50 Muslim countries. Iran and Sudan are two Muslim countries that operate wholly Shariah compliant banking systems. By the end of 2015, there were a total of 11 jurisdictions in which Islamic banking industry had a share of 15% or more in the whole banking industry. The major OIC jurisdictions also include Saudi Arabia, Bahrain, UAE, and Malaysia (the leaders in the industry), and Pakistan, Indonesia, Bangladesh, Jordan, Qatar, Bahrain, Kuwait, Turkey, Yemen, Brunei, Thailand, Algeria, Azerbaijan, Kenya, Oman, Lebanon, and Tunisia. Of these, Saudi Arabia, Malaysia, Yemen, Kuwait, Bangladesh, and UAE have a substantial share (18–50%) of

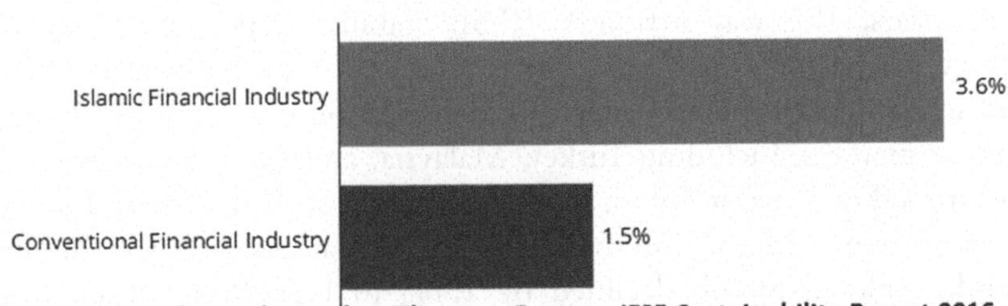

Fig. 1 Islamic finance status. *Source* Bloomberg, The Banker, Thomson Reuters, IFSB Sustainability Report 2016

Islamic banking in their overall banking industry. More recently, countries such as Maldives, Palestine, and Djibouti (in Africa) have also entered the landscape.

Today, Islamic banking or Islamic finance is no longer targeted at only Muslim populations, with its presence in major non-Muslim countries such as United Kingdom (one of the earliest leaders in the industry with London as one of the four major Islamic finance hubs), Singapore, Nigeria, South Africa, Sri Lanka, etc. Other states such as Germany, China in particular (with Hong Kong entering Islamic capital markets hub), the USA, Canada, and Australia have also shown a growing interest in the Islamic banking or Islamic capital markets industry.

The Islamic finance industry is deemed inherently asset based with risk-sharing instruments such as Mudarabah and Musharakah and claims to be more financially stable than the recently fragile (albeit recovering) conventional system. The industry has seen phenomenal growth at the global level in the last three decades, though this has not come without several challenges and emerging areas of concern. Today, there are over 700 IFIs operating in the world, in approximately 50 Muslim countries (including Bahrain, Malaysia, UK, and Iran as the leaders, and Saudi Arabia, UAE, Sudan, Indonesia, Pakistan, Bangladesh, Jordan, Qatar, Oman, Kuwait etc.) and over 40 non-Muslim countries including the UK (with London as one of the main Islamic finance centers), USA, South Africa, Canada, Australia, Switzerland, and Sri Lanka), with recent initiatives to launch Islamic banking in countries like China and Germany. Though it started as an economic need for faith-based (Muslim) investors, consumers, corporations, and governments, today, Islamic finance is no longer exclusive to Muslims. It is often seen as a form of ethical banking and investing (with the legal guidelines based on Islamic law) and a possibly stable/less risky alternative mode of financing by the non-Muslim world.

The size of the global Islamic finance industry has traditionally been measured in terms of the value of the assets held by institutions considered as a part of the Islamic finance industry. The size (June 2016) was estimated at between $1.88 trillion and $2.1 trillion, with the market size expected to reach more than $3.4 trillion by the end of the year 2018.[3]

Breakdown of Islamic Finance Segments by Region (USD billion, 2015 YTD*)

Region	Banking Assets	*Sukūk* Outstanding	Islamic Funds' Assets	*Takāful* Contributions
Asia	209.3	174.7	23.2	5.2
GCC	598.8	103.7	31.2	10.4
MENA (exc. GCC)	607.5	9.4	0.3	7.1
Sub-Saharan Africa	24.0	0.7	1.4	0.5
Others	56.9	2.1	15.2	-
Total	1496.5	290.6	71.3	23.2

**Data for banking and takāful as of 1H2015, while for sukūk and funds as of 11M15.*
Source: IFSB Secretariat Workings.

Fig. 2 Breakdown of Islamic finance. *Source* IFSB Annual Stability Report 2016

However, such figures generally underestimate the size of the industry, as they do not consider Islamic equities as an asset class. According to the Islamic Financial Services Board (IFSB)'s annual stability report, the total value of the global Islamic financial market industry was US$1.88 trillion by the year 2015. The table below shows the breakdown by segments. As the table demonstrates, the total value of the banking assets, outstanding Sukuk, Islamic funds' assets, and Takaful contributions for the year 2015 are US$1.881 trillion.

Recent sovereign Sukuk issues include Malaysia, which issued a Murabaha Sukuk on September 30, 2016, to raise RM 2 billion with a 19-year tenure, and Turkey, which on September 28, 2016, raised 2.16 billion lira (US$726 million) by issuing two 2-year lira-denominated Sukuk bonds (Fig. 2).

3 Islamic Finance in Pakistan

An initiative to re-launch Islamic banking in Pakistan started in the early 2000, as a long-term plan to shift the financial system to an interest-free economy, but through a gradual, market-driven and flexible approach, without major disruptions. The government of Pakistan decided to promote Islamic banking as a parallel and compatible system.

Islamic banking was re-introduced in Pakistan in 2002, with Meezan as its first licensed Islamic bank. Today, there are a total of 22 Islamic banks operating in Pakistan. The market share of Islamic banking assets stood at 11.8% in September 2016, with the market shares in terms of deposits at 13.3%.[4]

Pakistan has an active Islamic Banking department at the State Bank of Pakistan (SBP), the Securities and Exchange Commission of Pakistan (SECP), and a Shariah Advisory Board at the SBP serving as the highest authority for IFIs in the country. There is a legal framework in place that is a combination of the Bahraini and Malaysian model, for any FI operating as (a) an Islamic commercial bank, (b) an Islamic subsidiary of a conventional bank, or (c) financially separate Islamic branches of a conventional bank (Islamic windows). A regulatory framework for Takaful (Islamic insurance) companies is also in practice. At present, there are five full-fledged Islamic banks operating in Pakistan (Meezan, AlBaraka, BankIslami, Dubai Islamic Bank, MCB Islamic—a subsidiary of Muslim Commercial Bank), and 17 conventional banks operating Islamic windows, including two (Faysal Bank Ltd. and Summit Bank) that have announced their intent to convert to full-fledged Islamic banks. Other conventional banks with Islamic branches include Bank of Khyber, Bank Al Habib, HBL, NBP, UBL, Askari Bank, Standard Chartered, BOP, Sindh Bank, and Habib Metro. There are also five Takaful companies operating in Pakistan (2015), though with no IFI offering re-Takaful products as yet. Though the Bahrain-based international AAOIFI standards for Accounting, Auditing, and Shariah are widely accepted by SBP and IFIs in Pakistan, their implementation is still in its initial stages.

In terms of size, there are about 1700 Islamic banking branches operating in Pakistan (as of June 2016, SBP Islamic Banking Bulletin), with Islamic banking assets totaling to PKR 1745 billion (11.4% market share of the industry) and total deposits of PKR 1461 billion (13.3% of the industry). The share of Islamic Banking assets in Pakistan, which was 12.8% (December 2015) of the total banking industry, rose to 13.3% by September 2016, and the figure is targeted to reach 20% by 2020. The deposits grew by 14.1% annually (June 2016). In fact, between 2010 and 2015, the Islamic banking industry experienced a compound annual growth of over 30% in terms of both assets and deposits (December 2015, Islamic Finance Country Report), and the growth rate since its inception (in 2002) has been approximately 35%. Diminishing Musharakah (35.8%) and Murabaha (20.1%) were the two most common financing modes for IFIs in 2015–2016. In the year September 2015–2016 alone, the deposits of the Islamic banking industry had shown an annual growth of 16.6%.

A significant factor with regard to the financial inclusion and facilities provided by Islamic banks in any country is the client-wise financing provided by Islamic banks. In Pakistan, the corporate sector was the main sector financed by Islamic banks by September 2016 (receiving 73.5% of overall Islamic banks' financing), with consumer financing standing second at 11.3% and commodity financing (e.g., through commodity Murabaha) being at 7.9%. It was noted, however, that despite their growth, the financing extended by Islamic banks to SMEs (2.8%) and agricultural sector (0.8%) remained small.[5] At the same time, however, in terms of non-performing financings (NPFs), Islamic banks did an overall better job than the conventional banking industry, with their gross NPF to financing ratio standing at only 5.6%, compared to the industry average of 11.3% (September 2016).

However, one persistent challenge faced by Islamic banks in Pakistan was the lack of Shariah compliant instruments, including sovereign instruments (e.g., Ijarah Sukuk and Bai Muajjal certificates) available in the market for IFIs' liquidity management. The State Bank of Pakistan reported that, in the quarter July–September 2016 alone, liquid assets of Islamic banking institutions increased by PKR 72 billion and were recorded at PKR 747 billion in total. Perhaps consequentially, the return on assets and return on equity ratios of Islamic banking institutions on average were significantly lower than the local industry average, recorded at 0.6% (compared to 1.3% for the industry) and 9.8% (14.2% for the industry), respectively.

The government of Pakistan (GoP) expressed the hope that this surplus liquidity of Islamic banks could be used to finance infrastructure development in Pakistan. Several diminishing Musharakah, Istisna, and Ijarah-based Sukuk structures have been used on a limited scale by a few Islamic banks for short- and medium-term Islamic financing, and with the $46 billion China–Pakistan Economic Corridor (CPEC) on the horizon, there are many long-term developmental projects in renewable energy, hydel power, motorways, Gwadar port infrastructure, etc. that need financing. However, competitive Shariah compliant long-term financing structures need to be developed for this. The nation's Finance Minister, Mr. Ishaq Dar, stated at the World Islamic Finance Forum, "There has been an instruction from the finance ministry that wherever there is need to raise funds the priority should be given to the Islamic finance system."

On the plus note, as a significant step toward enhancing industry participation and general awareness about Islamic finance in Pakistan, the year 2016 saw the World Islamic Finance Forum (WIFF), organized by IBA Centre for Excellence in Islamic Finance (CEIF), held on September 5–6 at the Movenpick Hotel in Karachi. A number of local and international experts from the Islamic finance industry and academia attended the conference and presented their papers.

In September 2016, the SBP also issued a circular that gave Islamic banks exemption from using KIBOR (the Karachi Interbank operating rate) as the benchmark rate for their participatory and Wakala (agency)-based financing products. This was a step toward developing a Shariah compliant pricing benchmark for the local industry. In the same year, to encourage corporations to become Shariah compliant, the SBP allowed a 2% tax rebate to all firms that could be certified as Shariah complaint in their activates.

In order to regulate Pakistan's capital markets and non-banking financial institutions, the Securities and Exchange Commission of Pakistan (SECP) was established in 1997. However, the SECP did not introduce its Islamic Finance Department in February 2015 (a centralized Shariah Board also exists for the SECP). In terms of the local development of the Islamic capital markets industry in Pakistan, The KMI-30 (Karachi Meezan Index) was one of the two Shariah compliant indices launched in 2008. The regulatory framework for Takaful in Pakistan was first introduced as Takaful Rules in 2005. This year saw the birth of the country's first Takaful company, Pak–Kuwait Takaful. By 2014, Takaful windows were established in Pakistan. As of December 2015, there were five Takaful operators in the country, with Takaful assets totaling PKR 12 billion (in 2014). Islamic asset management first appeared in Pakistan in 2003, and by 2015, the total mutual funds were worth PKR 415 billion, with Shariah compliant fund assets totaling PKR 1053 billion. Islamic asset management first appeared in Pakistan in 2003. By June 2015, the total Shariah compliant fund assets amounted to PKR 1053 billion. Pakistan also established its Non-Banking Financial Institutions (NBFI) and Modaraba Association in

2010. By the end of 2014, there were 22 Modaraba companies, 10 leasing companies, and three investment banks operating in the country.[6]

The SECP issued Sukuk rules in the year 2015. The government of Pakistan entered the Sukuk market in June 2014, with the issue of a PKR 49.5 billion Ijarah Sukuk. Later in November 2014, it entered the international Islamic Sukuk market with its first foreign currency Sukuk issue: a 5-year Ijarah Sukuk of US$1 billion. This was at a profit rate of 6.75% (50 basis points less than the rate offered on Eurobond in April 2014) and was pledged against the Islamabad–Lahore Motorway. This attracted a wide international investor base, with 35% subscriptions from Europe, 32% from the Middle East, and 20% from North America. In December 2015, the GoP (government of Pakistan) issued a local currency Ijarah Sukuk, this time on the Jinnah Airport Terminal in Karachi, to raise PKR 300 billion (US$2.86 billion, about 14 times greater than the Britain Sukuk). This provided the local Islamic FIs with much-needed investment opportunities in government securities, as they had about PKR 225–220 billion in excess liquidity at the time, unable to invest in the conventional Treasury bills and government securities and hence being at a significant disadvantage with the local conventional finance industry.

WAPDA (Pakistan's Water and Power Development Authority) then issued a 10-year PKR 100 billion Sukuk on the Neelum–Jhelum Hydropower Plant (NJHP) in April 2016, to raise finance for the hydel project. This was rated at 0.113 basis points over the 6-month KIBOR and was backed by a sovereign guarantee from the GoP. Private corporations in Pakistan can also issue Sukuk, with the legal framework developed by the Islamic Banking Department of the SBP. K-Electric issued a PKR 22 billion 7-year Musharakah–Sukuk in May 2015 to help repay its long-term debt via the Karachi Stock Exchange, with HBL and Meezan Bank as its lead arrangers, and this was reportedly the largest listed corporate Sukuk in the country at the time. In October 2016, the GoP issued another foreign currency 5-year sovereign Ijarah-Sukuk of US$1 billion.[7] By the end of 2015, Pakistan had outstanding Sukuk worth US$2.92 billion and outstanding Islamic mutual funds' assets worth US$1.32 billion.[8]

For regulatory Shariah compliance, the State Bank of Pakistan, since the re-start of Islamic banking in Pakistan in 2003, put a high-powered Shariah Board in place to advise the SBP on Shariah-related matters. This board consists of six members: three Shariah scholars, one lawyer, one accountant, and one banker. It reviews and approves the Shariah compliance of the Islamic finance instruments and advises SBP in prudential regulations set up by the Islamic banking sector in Pakistan. SBP's Commission for Transformation of the Financial System, set up after a historic Supreme Court Judgment on Riba on 23rd December 1999, has approved structures of Islamic finance modes including Mudarabah, Musharakah, Murabaha, Musawama, Ijarah, Salam, and Istisna. The SBP also released a detailed Shariah governance framework for Islamic banks in 2014.

Today, Pakistan has a regulatory framework in place for full-fledged Islamic banking institutions, Islamic subsidiaries of conventional banks, and Islamic banking windows (stand-alone Islamic banking branches of existing conventional banks). With sixteen conventional banks in Pakistan operating 860 Islamic banking windows (September 2016),[9] and over 1300 branches of five full-fledged Islamic banks, Islamic banking and finance in Pakistan has seen tremendous growth in the last 13 years. However, the industry is faced with several key challenges in the face of its long-term vision of converted to a fully Shariah compliant and efficient financial system. For one, the financial inclusion in the economy is very less, with a large percentage of unbanked population. For another, the levels of awareness about Riba, Islamic banking, and its principles are very less, in the masses, educated population, and sometimes even among employees and customers of Islamic banks. For this purpose, now many universities and Madrassas (Islamic learning educational institutes) in Pakistan have included Islamic banking and finance courses as part of their curriculum. Also, the SBP helped set up three Centers of Excellence in Islamic finance, in IBA (Karachi), Lahore University of Management Sciences, and IM Sciences, Peshawar (KPK Province), with the greater objective of raising the awareness levels about Islamic banking, provide research and industry collaborations, and help produce the much-needed trained human resources to develop the Islamic finance industry and support its growth.

Additionally, there is a greater need for some financial innovation in Pakistan's Islamic finance industry. For instance, there is still no re-Takaful operator in Pakistan. With only limited Shariah compliant GoP securities and Sukuk, investment options for IFIs' liquidity management are severely limited. Islamic banking products more suited to the SMEs and rural agricultural sector are also needed.

4 What Does the Future Hold?

One of the major challenges of the Islamic finance is the disruption caused by fin-tech and the need for innovative branchless banking methods that best caters to the needs of the population. Though a large fraction of the banked population in GCC countries comprises of educated people, with high levels of income with a very developed mobile usage (hence a very fertile ground for mobile banking), the concept of digital banking is only just emerging in the GCC, and Islamic financial institutions have to provide innovative solutions to adapt to this change. According to the Ernst and Young World Islamic Banking Competitiveness Report (2016), 98% of their surveyed banked customers were smartphone users, with at least 72% using their phones for daily messaging. The future of retail Islamic banking in the GCC hence includes a smartphone banking experience that delights the customers. Though mobile banking has indeed been started by Islamic banks in many countries, it has not fully taken off. For instance, EY reports that (by 2014), conventional banks appeared to have a competitive edge over Islamic banks in mobile banking, with 38% of their customers using mobile banking, compared to only 26% of Islamic banking customers (countries in the surveys included Bahrain, Kuwait, Qatar, UAE, Saudi Arabia, and Oman). Additionally, only less than half of the customers were satisfied with their mobile banking experience: only 34% in Saudi Arabia, 45% in UAE, 42% in Qatar, 50% in

Kuwait, etc. Common complaints included lack or difficulty in accessing their accounts, slow transaction speeds, no adaptability to consumers (e.g., ATMs asking the customer even after 10 years what was their language preference), and the apps and products not being tailored to the consumers' needs.

Furthermore, as the Islamic finance industry grows beyond the GCC and Southeast Asia, there is a greater need for Shariah compliant products' innovation, particularly in the case if Islamic derivative products that are needed by IFIs to hedge their risks. One recent development was the International Islamic Financial Market (IIFM)'s launching standard templates for Shariah complaint foreign exchange forward, as an attempt to improve the hedging practices in the global Islamic financial sector. This could be an effective tool for managing foreign currency risks for IFIs.

Another challenge for Islamic finance and the Islamic banking industry in many countries is that of financial inclusion. Given that many segments of the Muslim populations across the globe seek banking and/or credit facilities only if they deem them compliant with their religious beliefs, Islamic banking should extend its facilities to the small and medium enterprises (SMEs) sector, for microfinance, for the agricultural sector, for branchless banking customers, and for the large unbanked sector in many OIC countries.

In some jurisdictions, Pakistan included, the Islamic finance industry faces the challenge of not having a level playing field with the conventional financial institutions. For instance, even though they compete in the same market, with very similar expectations from depositors and shareholders in terms of profit rates, ROA, ROE, etc., and IFIs are additionally restricted in being able to only invest in Shariah compliant securities in the capital markets, they generally have the same regulatory requirements, in terms of capital reserves, CRR, SLR, etc., as conventional institutions. Sometimes, there is a shortage of Shariah compliant government securities to invest in, and this hampers the profitability of the IFIs.

Last, but not the least, Islamic finance in each market can only be as successful as the level of awareness in that market about Islamic banking and finance.

Notes

1. 'Maqasid Al Shariah: An Introductory Guide', by Jasser Auda (2008). Pages 11–22.
2. CEIF, King Fahad University of Petroleum and Minerals.
3. 'The Size of the Islamic Finance Market', June 2016, Islamicfinance.com.
4. 'State Bank of Pakistan Islamic Banking Bulletin,' September 2016.
5. SBP Islamic Banking Bulletin, September 2016.
6. Pakistan Islamic Finance Country Report 2016 by IBA CEIF, Thomson Reuters, and IRTI, pages 10–16.
7. Source: Sukuk.com Web site.
8. Pakistan Islamic Finance Country Report 2016, pages 56–57.
9. State Bank of Pakistan 'Islamic Banking Bulletin,' September 2016, pages 20.

Reference

Islamic Financial Services Board (IFSB)'s Stability Report, May 2016.

Sukuk for the Financing of Non-revenue Water Management: Malaysia as a Case Study

Kulsanofer Syed Thajudeen

Abstract Water is essential for life, and it is increasingly becoming scarce. The World Economic Forum's Global Risks 2015 report stated that global water crises are the biggest threat facing the planet over the next decade. Despite the fact that water scarcity is going to be a global issue, a staggering 32 billion cubic meters of treated water is lost to urban supply systems around the world. The World Bank reported that more than US$14 billion is lost every year by water utilities worldwide, more than a third of that by water utilities in developing countries. By reducing the water loss, 8 billion cubic meters per year of treated water can provide water to an additional 90 million people who currently lack access to clean potable water. The terminology often used for the water that is lost is non-revenue water (NRW). NRW is basically the difference between the amount of water supplied to the distribution system and the amount of water billed to consumers. Water is lost through leaking pipes or theft. Eliminating NRW altogether is not feasible,

K.S. Thajudeen (✉)
INCEIF, Kuala Lumpur, Malaysia
e-mail: kulsanofer@gmail.com

S.A.R. Rizvi and I. Saba (eds.), *Developments in Islamic Finance*, Palgrave CIBFR Studies in Islamic Finance, DOI 10.1007/978-3-319-59342-5_2

though reducing the current level to half is a reasonable target in most developing countries. Although the NRW issue is a global phenomenon, it can only be understood and acted based on its local conditions. For that reason, Malaysia is taken as a case study. The NRW problem is an issue for the water utilities in Malaysia as some states lose nearly 60% of their treated water (MWIG 2015). The water utilities do not spend on NRW management, as the cost of maintenance is higher than the revenue received from consumers due to low tariffs. This research studies the feasibility of using sukuk to finance the NRW problem in Malaysia. The methodology used is a cost-benefit analysis. The results indicate saving water through leakage preventions is a profitable venture with benefits amounting to RM2.13 bil/year and able to service additional 26.8 million people. This study defines the benefits of reducing NRW in terms of value and solving the issue through structuring Green Sukuk to finance NRW work. Due to the universality of the issue, the sukuk structure could be replicated with specificities related to each country. The limitation of the study is that it only looks at part of the NRW, which is the physical losses, and not into apparent losses, which includes theft and meter inaccuracies.

Keywords Water resources · Risk sharing · Islamic countries · Malaysia

1 Introduction

Water is the elixir of life, and it is crucial for the survival of living beings. Although water covers 70% of the planet, the available freshwater only makes up 1% of the total water. Another 2% is in the form of frozen glaciers or otherwise unable for use. In essence, only 0.007% of the planet's water is available to fuel and feed its 6.8 billion people (Shiklomanov 1993).

Most of the freshwater are in the form of rivers and lakes, and these have become stressed with growing populations. The Colorado River, Indus River, Yellow River, and Murray River are among the rivers that have been overused, with the rivers drying up before reaching the sea (Inman 2010). Water is overdrawn for irrigation and industrial and household use.

If overconsumption of water is not bad enough, climate change is also contributing toward water security challenges. Many developing countries have to cope with droughts and floods, which would make water difficult and costly to distribute. Currently, 1.6 billion people live in countries and regions with absolute water scarcity, and the number is expected to rise to 2.8 billion people by 2025 (Alavian et al. 2009).

In fact, the World Economic Forum's Global Risks 2015 report stated that global water crises are the biggest threat facing the planet over the next decade, and for the first time, water was placed at the top, as the most impactful risk to economies, environments, and people. This is because of the nexus of water with food and energy. The success of the other sectors is tied closely with the existence of water. The GWP/OECD *Global Dialogue on Water Security and Sustainable Growth* (Sadoff et al. 2015) provides evidence that water security is much more than a component of wider economic goals; rather, it has a crucial influence on the nature and speed of wider economic development. Strategic water investment decisions can open up opportunities for economic development. Sustained investment in water infrastructure and its "enabling environment" is an essential pillar for growing economies.

The coming decades will see a convergence of growing populations, rising incomes, and a changing climate. Demand for water will increase throughout all sectors of the economy, while, at the same time, water supplies will become more variable and less predictable. Indeed, estimates suggest that within the next three decades, the global food system will require between 40 and 50% more water; municipal and industrial water demand will increase by 50–70%; the energy sector will see water demand increase by 85%; and the environment, already the residual claimant, may receive even less. The costs of policy inaction are high, and prudent stewardship of water resources will pay large dividends (World Bank 2016).

The problem is the distribution and stewardship of water. Much of the world's water is used inefficiently by industry, agriculture, and cities even in arid areas; much of it is wasted without economic benefit, often with negative environmental impacts. In fact, a staggering 32 billion cubic meters of treated water is lost to urban supply systems around the world each year through physical leaks in the pipes. Half of these losses occur in developing countries where customers already frequently suffer from interrupted supplies and poor water quality (Kingdom et al. 2006).

1.1 Non-revenue Water (NRW)

Water that is lost is known as non-revenue water (NRW). According to the International Water Association (IWA), NRW is water that has been produced and is "lost" before it reaches the customer. Losses can be real losses (through leaks, sometimes also referred to as physical losses) or apparent losses (e.g., through theft or metering inaccuracies). Refer to Fig. 1.

The low water tariff is one of the main reasons for the inefficiency of the water utilities. There is no incentive for the utilities to prevent wastage, as they cannot recover the cost of fixing leaks in the system. Cheap water condones consumer behavior toward wastage instead of conservation of water. If the current consumption rate continues alongside the inefficiency of water distribution, by 2025, nearly two-thirds of the world population will face water shortage. If the water utilities in developing countries just reduce NRW by half the current level, 8 billion cubic meters of treated water would be available to service 90 million people without stressing the water sources. An additional of US$2.9 billion can be gained by fixing the leaks without the necessity of building more water infrastructure to meet water demands (ibid.).

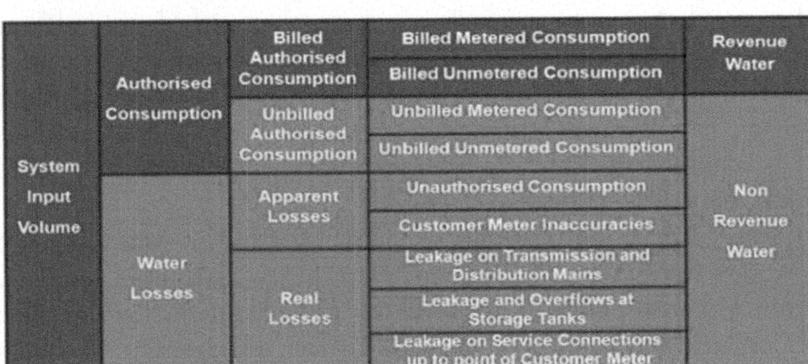

Fig. 1 Standard IWA water balance

Although the water crisis is a global phenomenon, it can only be understood and acted upon based on its local conditions (WEF 2009). Thus, for the purpose of this research, Malaysia is taken as a case study. The proposed research is to study the inefficiencies of water distribution in Peninsular Malaysia and conduct a cost-benefit analysis of financing a nationwide water loss reduction program. Sukuk is to be structured to finance this program. The intention behind the financing is very much in line with the Shariah principles, which is to safeguard the environment for the mutual benefit of all. This could be an avenue to issue Malaysia's first Green Sukuk.

1.2 NRW in Malaysia

Malaysia has had several water crises over the years. The country with a population of 30 million and a growth rate of 1.5% consists of 14 states. The water crisis occurred again in April this year, with dams especially in the northern states of Perak, Penang, Kedah, and Perlis drying up. The Linggiu Reservoir in Johor, which also supplies water to Singapore, was only one-third full (The Star 2016). The Bukit Merah Dam in Perak, Malaysia's oldest dam, hovered at 6 m, while the normal storage level for full water supply is 8.7 m, way below the "danger" level of 40%. The Ulu Muda River which supplies 96% of treated water supply to Kedah and 80% to Penang is running dry. While El Nino, which has been the strongest yet with months-long heat wave, is the cause of the dying of dams and rivers, excessive deforestation and mismanagement of the dams are other factors exacerbating the problem. It is rather ironic that for a country with rainfall of nearly 3000 mm per year, a nationwide water rationing was exercised affecting millions of consumers, not to mention the financial loss to the agricultural and other industries (Yeh 2016).

Another important factor is the high NRW water issue in the country. The NRW problem has been plaguing water utilities in Malaysia for decades. In some states, the NRW is as high as 56%, while the national average is at 38% (MWIG 2015). Increasing the number of water treatment plants will not solve the water security problem if 50% of the water treated is lost through leaking pipes. The high NRW levels indicate the inefficiency of the water utilities, and for developing countries, the first step would be to reduce NRW levels while addressing the higher demand for water (Dighade et al. 2015). The water operators are unable to solve their NRW problem due to the insufficient revenue due to low water tariffs. Thus, the water operators have no incentive to spend on maintenance and operations of their assets.

An important point to note is that the NRW management is not a one-time activity. Although an intense and comprehensive NRW reduction program is suitable to reduce the backlog of required NRW reduction measures, it will not lead to a sustainable low level of NRW unless NRW management becomes part of the normal day-to-day activities of the water utility (Frauendorfer and Liemberger 2010). Thus, in order to successfully reduce the NRW issue in the country, a structured long-term holistic program must be in place, involving all the crucial players like the regulators, water operators, financiers, and contractors.

1.3 NRW in Pakistan

Pakistan is among the world's 36 most water-stressed countries despite having the world's largest glaciers. With a population of 189 million and a growth rate of 1.49% (World Bank 2016), the demand for water would definitely increase, and the drop in per capita annual water availability from 5600 m^3 in 1947 to the current level of 1017 m^3 is not encouraging. There is a growing concern regarding the demand and supply gap (IMF 2015), and the recent study by the Pakistan Council of Research in Water Resources (PCRWR) warned that the country can run dry by 2025 if necessary actions are not taken (Wasif 2016).

There are ten water operators providing water to the four provinces. The Karachi Water and Sewerage Board is the biggest water utility, and the NRW in Karachi is around 30–35%. The Capital Development Authority (CDA), Islamabad, provides water without any meters, and the NRW is estimated as 32%. At the Water and Sanitation Agency (WASA), Gujranwala, the NRW is estimated as 60%. The reasons for these are mostly due to water theft, aging infrastructure, and system leakage. Not much work has been done on NRW due to financial constraints (Shoail et al. 2014). The water problem in Pakistan is slightly different from Malaysia because most of the NRW issue is caused by water theft. The first step to solve the NRW problem is to install meters for billing purposes, and also to have accurate NRW data.

1.4 Water in Islam

The Quran gives much emphasis to water with 63 verses with the word (ÁÇã mā'), which means water in Arabic, and even the meaning of Shariah or Islamic jurisprudence is the "way to the watering hole." There is some quality of spirituality in this natural resource that God bestows as a gift to man. It can be witnessed in the religious rituals of many religions of the world, from Hinduism as devotees bath in sacred rivers like the Ganges to the act of baptism in Christianity and ritual purification in Judaism, Shintoism, and Zoroastrianism. In Islam, water plays an important part in religious purification before the obligatory prayers.

The themes in the Quran regarding water emphasize its importance: for example, water is the building block of living things: "We made every living thing from water" (20:30); rain as mercy and a provision to mankind: "It is He who sends down water for you from the sky, from which comes a drink for you, and the shrubs that you feed to your animals. With it He grows for you grain, olives, palms, vines and all kinds of other crops. There truly is a sign in this for those who reflect." (16:10–11). This is the main theme that is often repeated in the Quran.

The famous Hadiths on water touch on conservation, preservation, i.e., prohibition of polluting water resources, and water rights. The Prophet (SAW) forbade the excessive use of water even when there was abundance flow. He (SAW) forbade the defiling of water sources with excrement. This is the origin of the concept of "harim" or buffer zone to protect water sources from pollution of human activities (Wickstrom 2010). The Hadith, "Men are co-owners in three things: water, fire and pastures," emphasizes the common rights of man toward water. The Hadith also encouraged the concept of prohibition of sale of water. However, according to the Maliki and Shafi'e mazhab, the owner of a supply of water can sell and dispose of it at will, except in the case of water in a well due to watering of livestock. The Maliki school of thought stipulates that the purpose of the sale must be known and stipulated. The Hanafi and Hanbali mazhab, on the other hand, only allow the sale of water in receptacles (Faruqui et al. 2001).

2 Literature Review

Global infrastructure demand requires USD 57 trillion in investment by 2030, and it is 60% more than the USD 36 trillion spent globally on infrastructure over the past 18 years (Dobbs et al. 2013). When analyzed by sector, water made up one of the largest contributors for expenditure (OECD 2007). The main reason behind this is the aging infrastructure like pipelines that distribute drinking water, and it is a common problem all over the world. Thames Water in London has the highest level of water leakage in the UK, and it has spent 11 billion over the years and the costs are expected to increase (London 2003). In the USA, the estimated cost of the capital investment to maintain and upgrade drinking water and wastewater treatment systems in 2010 is USD 91 billion. However, only USD 36 billion of this USD 91 billion needed was funded, leaving a capital funding gap of nearly USD 55 billion (ASCE 2011).

Lloyd Owen (2009) forecasted the spending needs both for investments and for operation and maintenance of water services, across 67 countries both developed and developing costs, as USD 2880 billion in investments over the next two decades. The associated operating costs could be twice as high as capital investment costs. According to the report by OECD (Infrastructure to 2030, 2007), there will be a growing infrastructure investment gap, and traditional public finance alone will not suffice to meet future infrastructure needs. The inability to bridge the infrastructure investment gap could result in costly consequences in the future. An even bigger effort is required to be directed toward the maintenance, routine repairs, and upgradation of existing infrastructure as this can minimize future investment needs.

Closing the water-financing gap will require countries to mobilize financing from a variety of sources, which may include reducing costs and increasing efficiency. The traditional sources of finance like tariffs, taxes, and transfers (commonly referred to as the "3Ts") may not be sufficient to close the financing gap. It was imperative to close the gap not only for economic growth but also to meet the United Nations Millennium Development Goals (MDG). Goal Seven of the MDG is to halve the proportion of people without access to sustainable safe drinking water by 2015.

The landmark reports, the Camdessus Report in 2003 (Winpenny 2003), and the Gurria Report in 2006 (Hofwegen 2006) prompted much interest in water financing. The Camdessus Report called for an increase in private sector participation in the water sector.

Financing water infrastructure means spending cash to finance long-term physical assets, which can only be reimbursed over time by users, taxpayers, or donors. Financing is required not just for investment needs but also for recurring expenditure on administrative overheads, operations, maintenance, routine repairs, and periodic replacements. A common assumption is that the revenues of water utilities cover these. But this is often not the case, and shortfalls on repairs and maintenance lead to a need for higher investment in due course. Up to a point, adequate budgeting for recurrent spending items, backed by good cost recovery, can minimize future investment needs.

The Gurria Report focused on innovative financing options for local governments, as they are not able to access financing due to lack of willingness at the national level, an absence of creditworthiness, and a lack of awareness. Moss et al. (2003) address some causes of underinvestment and operational neglect in the water sector whether it is public or privately owned. Water-related infrastructure requires significant levels of investment and has long payback periods. The failure to recognize the full value of water services makes it difficult to mobilize funds resulting in inadequate investments and maintenance. The indirect benefits to health, economic growth, and environmental quality are not recognized. The lack of priority given to water sector by political leaders and the belief that increased expenditure will not result in better services are other reasons.

There was a lot of emphasis on privatization of water services in the 1990s advocated by international financial institutions (IFIs) such as the World Bank, regional development banks, and bilateral donor agencies. The pro-privatization policies and practices are reinforced by the Organization for Economic Corporation and Development (OECD), the World Trade Organization (WTO), and multinational corporations. The Water Resources Management Policy states that water should be treated as an economic commodity, with an emphasis on efficiency, financial discipline, and full cost recovery, including profits. The World Bank since then has promoted privatization as a solution to the water supply and sanitation crisis (World Bank 2004a, b, c).

Privatization of water and sanitation services has many variations like concessions, management and lease contracts, service contracts, and public–private partnerships (PPPs). PPP is where the operating company is a joint venture between the public owner of the assets and the private company, which usually has a form of management control over the utility. Marin et al. (2009) analyzed performance data for more than 65 large water PPP projects. The study concludes that the main effects of PPPs have been significant improvements in operational efficiency. There is an ongoing debate regarding PPPs and privatization of water utilities, and studies show that privatization is not always successful (Lobina et al. 2014).

The emphasis should be more on innovative finance mechanism to bridge the financing gap in the water sector regardless of whether it is a public or private entity. Traditionally, there are three basic sources of revenues for water services: tariffs, taxation, and transfers also commonly known as 3Ts. (OECD 2009). Market-based repayable finance, referring to loans, bonds, and equities, can be provided to either public or private operators (see Fig. 2). For example, in the USA, municipal bonds subscribed by private investors largely financed municipal public operators. In England, the artesian loan facility was created to allow smaller water-only companies (WOCs) access to bond finance as it is cheaper than commercial bank finance. The artesian loan facility provides an "umbrella" under which the WOCs can group together

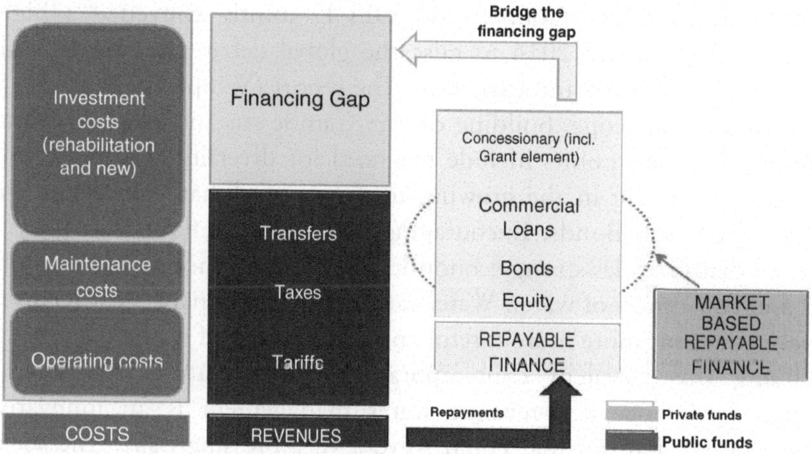

Fig. 2 Market based repayable finance. *Source* OECD (2010), innovative finance mechanisms for the water sector, OECD, Paris

to issue debt at cheaper conditions. The credit quality of the combined bond issue is guaranteed by a "monoline insurer," which guarantees the bondholders' demands in the case of failure of one of the firms in the loan structure. Investor security is further enhanced by disclosure agreements and by isolating water revenues from other interests in the company. This facility allows small companies with large capital expenditure requirements to raise the required financing at very preferential terms (OECD 2010).

Operation and maintenance is one area that is often neglected due to the financing gap. This results in operation inefficiency. Non-revenue water is one of the largest inefficiencies in the water utilities. An estimate of nearly US$14 billion is wasted each year in lost revenue. In developing countries, almost 45 million cubic meters of treated water leaks daily from urban water supply systems (Kingdom et al. 2006). Innovative financing mechanism can be utilized to fund maintenance of aging infrastructure, as the basic 3T revenues are not sufficient. Reducing water loss is beneficial not only to the water operators to increase revenues but also to the environment as water resources are not stressed.

The World Water Council and OECD jointly convened a high-level panel (HLP) in 2014 to raise the global debate on how to scale up financing of water infrastructure. The report (Winpenny et al. 2015) covered a broad scope, building on the Camdessus and Gurria reports. Among the main points include the need for diversity and innovation in water financing in the growing resources of climate funds and the growth of Green Bonds. Encouraging innovation to flourish requires a regime that provides strong economic and financial incentives to suppliers and consumers of water. Water tariffs set at sustainable cost recovery levels would promote more careful and efficient use of water.

Using the prevalent contemporary Islamic financial instrument, sukuk, to finance non-revenue water management is an innovative financing mechanism that could solve a very pressing issue. The social and environmental benefits in reducing water loss are very much in line with Islamic law which contains a deeply entrenched ethical framework of concern for the environment and its diverse inhabitants. In fact, a Green Sukuk can be structured, as water loss reduction is one of the criteria for issuing of a Green Bond. It further demonstrates the commitment of Islamic finance to the environment and expands the common ground with SRI markets (Moghul and Safar-Aly 2015).

In order to enable the sukuk to be commercially viable, cost recovery is an important feature in reforming tariff structures (World Bank 2003). Cost recovery is achieved when a service provider is able to bring in sufficient revenues from customers to cover their current and future costs. These include operations and maintenance costs (to deliver the services) as well as capital costs (including recuperation of asset depreciation over time and savings to pay for future capital investment needs (Rodriguez et al. 2012). In order to achieve cost recovery, the water rates need to be reviewed. Historically, water rates have been insufficient in covering long-run costs (Levin and Epstein et al. 2002). A well-designed pricing system can encourage conservation, reduce demand and requirements for future infrastructure expansion, and accommodate the long-run costs of the system.

Offering a commercially viable Green Sukuk for the maintenance of water infrastructure is a way of empowering the public in the management of the water utilities and securing better water quality for all.

3 Methodology

The literature on the finances of NRW reduction and control programs is abundant. It includes studies on results, costs, and benefits of leak detection and repair programs and models on the finances of NRW. Walski (1984) explored the benefits of leak detection and repair programs, looking at both short-run and long-run cost savings. A study by Griffin (1983) showed that benefit/cost ratios range from 0.5 to 10 and are highest when the costs of water and initial leakage are high. The British Manual Leakage Control Policy and Practice (National Water Commission [NWC]) documents the impacts, costs, and benefits of various leakage control strategies. The key elements of NWC derive the unit cost of leakage, expected levels of leakage, various unit costs of different leakage control strategies that are estimated on a cost-per-property basis, find optimum level of leakage, and keep total system leakage low. Shore (1988) proposed a three-part formula for total cost of leakage: (1) cost of leakage, (2) cost of detection, and (3) repair cost, independent of the level of leakage. Later research included other parameters like flow rates, pressure, types of pipes, burst frequencies, fixed and variable area discharges, and unavailable to finally produce the short-run economic level of leakage (ELL) method which outlines the financially optimum level of physical losses. Other models concentrate on costs and benefits of reducing commercial losses (water theft) by analyzing the cost of water lost through failed or inaccurate meters.

In order to perform a cost-benefit analysis of the NRW loss reduction program, the important step is to decide on the costs and benefits to include, how they will be valued, the discounting rate, and the constraints involved. For the purpose of this study, the approach used is by converting the NRW expressed in percentage of system input volume to financial values using the corresponding unit value for water and deducting it with the costs of repairing leaks. The main objective is to provide evidence that repairing the leaks and saving the said amount of water, which is lost, make financial sense for the utility. Since 70% of the NRW problem arises from leakages in Malaysia, the emphasis was given to leakage prevention and not on commercial losses (Ranhill). The benefit would be increased or surplus revenue from the water losses. The intangible benefits include reduced stress on aquatic ecosystems as the water that is saved can be used to supply to more people. Other costs that are difficult to quantify are the opportunity cost of depriving willing buyers of quality water, the environmental stress and degradation due to excessive water demand, water evaporation from reservoirs, and water lost that equates to less water in the future (Zetland 2016).

For the purpose of this paper, the cost and benefit can be stated as below:

$$B = R - [C1 + C2] \tag{1}$$

B = annual benefit from conducting an NRW reduction program, RM/year;
R = annual possible revenue from water saved from NRW reduction, RM/year;
C1 = cost of repairing leaks, RM/year;
C2 = cost of surveying for leaks, RM/year;

$$R = NRW \times Revenue \tag{2}$$

NRW = Volume of Non-Revenue Water, Million Liters Per Day (MLD)
= System Input Volume − Billed Authorized Consumption
Revenue = average revenue per water billed (ARWB), RM/m^3

$$C1 = \text{Pipe Burst/Breakages/Leak (leak/year)} \times \text{Cost per Leak (RM/leak)} \tag{3}$$

$$C2 = \text{Length of pipes (Km)} \times \text{Cost of surveying (RM/Km/year)} \tag{4}$$

The Malaysian Water Association publishes an annual Malaysian Water Industry Guide (MWIG) with data on volume of NRW losses per year and other relevant data. The cost for repairing leaks and surveying was obtained from Ranhill Utilities Sdn Bhd, a private company that specializes in NRW work.

The 2014 data were used for this model. The apparent cost of losses was not included in this model because it only accounts for 30% of the

Table 1 2014 data from the MWIG

State	NRW (MLD)	ARWB (RM/m³)	Leakage	Cost per leak[a] (RM/leak)	Length of pipes (km)	Cost of survey[a] (RM/km/year)
Johor	426	1.88	61,525	500	20,898	400
Kedah	596	1.09	40,357	500	11,770	400
Kelantan	220	1.10	16,257	500	6698	400
Labuan	20	0.89	893	500	506	400
Melaka	102	1.26	24,712	500	4851	400
N. Sembilan	267	1.02	29,180	500	8575	400
P. Pinang	182	0.78	43,517	500	4335	400
Pahang	588	0.77	2471	500	10,307	400
Perak	379	0.99	39,322	500	11,325	400
Perlis	121	0.97	7456	500	1877	400
Sabah	618	1.07	18,050	500	15,031	400
Sarawak	381	0.84	16,769	500	11,797	400
Selangor	1545	1.49	136,163	500	27,251	400
Terengganu	188	0.77	20,282	500	8397	400
Total	5633		456,954		143,618	

[a]Information from Ranhill Utilities Sdn Bhd

losses, while 70% is from physical losses. Furthermore, there is insufficient data on apparent losses(Tables 1, 2).

The results indicate that the benefits from the NRW loss reduction program can reap up to **RM2.13 bil/year,** while the cost of the program is only a total **of RM 286 mil/year**. By reducing the losses, the utility can supply the additional water to **26.8 million** people (based on the average of 207 liters per capita per day system input). However, reducing NRW to 0% is not economically feasible. The reasonable target of the NRW reduction is around 20%, although in countries such as Singapore and Japan, they have achieved 4 and 8%, respectively (IBNet Database). Another important factor to note is that the cost of reducing apparent losses was not included in this study. For a more accurate study, the cost of commercial losses should be included.

In the case of Pakistan, more emphasis should be on the costs of apparent loss as the majority of the NRW cases involve water theft and the lack of meters. The cost of meter replacement and installation must be included to provide a better estimate of the cost-benefit analysis.

Table 2 The cost-benefit analysis for NRW loss reduction in Malaysia

State	R (RM/year)	C1(RM/year)	C2 (RM/year)	B
Johor	292,321,200	30,762,500	8,359,200	253,199,500
Kedah	237,118,600	20,178,500	4,708,000	212,232,100
Kelantan	88,330,000	8,128,500	2,679,200	77,522,300
Labuan	6,497,000	446,500	202,400	5,850,100
Melaka	46,909,800	12,356,000	1,940,400	32,613,400
N. Sembilan	99,404,100	14,590,000	3,430,000	81,384,100
P. Pinang	51,815,400	21,758,500	1,734,000	28,322,900
Pahang	165,257,400	1,235,500	4,122,800	159,899,100
Perak	136,951,650	19,661,000	4,530,000	112,760,650
Perlis	42,840,050	3,728,000	750,800	38,361,250
Sabah	241,359,900	9,025,000	6,012,400	226,322,500
Sarawak	116,814,600	8,384,500	4,718,800	103,711,300
Selangor	840,248,250	68,081,500	10,900,400	761,266,350
Terengganu	52,837,400	10,141,000	3,358,800	39,337,600
Total	**2,418,705,350**	228,477,000	**57,445,200**	2,132,783,150

4 Sukuk Structures

Sukuk structures are usually fully asset-based structures. However, over the years, sukuk structures have become more asset-light as well as industry-specific structures. There have been several industry-specific structures such as in the airline and the telecommunications industries. Airlines such as the Emirates and Garuda have used "travel rights" as the underlying asset for issuing sukuk, while telecommunications issuers like Ooredoo have used "airtime vouchers." In this case, "water rights" structure is to be used as the underlying asset. It is an innovative structure that can be duplicated in other countries to solve a very pressing issue at hand, which is the non-revenue water phenomenon.

The water sector in Malaysia includes the National Water Services Commission (SPAN), the state water corporation, the state water regulators, and PAAB, which is the national water asset-holding company. PAAB is the water sector financier with responsibilities that includes revenue and lease management, procurement, business planning, and water infrastructure development. The financial mechanism adopted by PAAB works on a build and lease platform. In principle, this concept gives PAAB the mandate to secure funding to develop water infrastructure and then lease this infrastructure to water utilities for an agreed

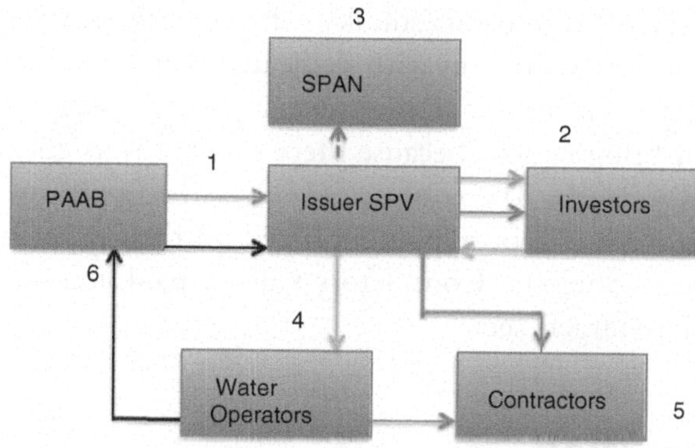

Fig. 3 The NRW loss reduction Green Sukuk

The NRW loss reduction Green Sukuk can be issued for a period of 20 years. The sukuk al-manafa'a- wakalah-ijarah structure consists of the following transactions

(1) The PAAB incorporates an SPV. The SPV, as issuer, issues the sukuk, representing ownership interest in the underlying asset, water rights

(2) The investors subscribe for the sukuk and pay the proceeds to the SPV, as issuer

(3) SPAN is declared as a guarantor for the investors and is under an obligation to make up any shortfall restoration amount

(4) Wakalah Agreement: The SPV hires the water operator as a wakil to undertake the oversight of the NRW contractors. The water operators receive wakalah fees

(5) Ijarah Agreement: The SPV hires the contractors to perform the NRW work

(6) The water operators collect all revenue gained from the NRW loss reduction work and pay PAAB. PAAB collects certain percentage for the water rights pledged. PAAB then transfers the remainder of revenue to the SPV who in turn pays the investors

lease rental. In order to structure sukuk, the originator would be PAAB. The water operators would be agents to perform the NRW loss reduction work with contractors, with the raised money. The National Water Services Commission would act as the guarantor for the investor (Fig. 3).

An advantage of having this sukuk is the centralized structured program for NRW loss reduction with dedicated teams to solve the problem. In the past, Government incentive to water operators to reduce NRW did not bring benefit because there was no oversight on expenditure and NRW levels. The contractors selected to perform the NRW loss reduction work will be appointed based on their expertise and performance-based contracts. Contractors will be paid according to their ability to achieve targets set.

5 Conclusion

The study shows that water scarcity is a significant problem that would affect a large part of the world. There is an important need to conserve water and reducing the NRW loss is something that all utilities worldwide can do. Unfortunately, utilities are unable to pay for the extensive cost of maintenance, as the revenue from billed water is insufficient to cover the costs. One of the reasons for this is because the water tariffs are too low to enable for the utilities to be self-sustainable. Innovative financing is required to finance this important exercise to ensure water security in the future. It is also important to spend on conserving rather than outsourcing for more water as that can lead to depleting available water sources. Islamic finance should be applied to provide the financing as it is very much in line with the Shariah principles. The study also shows that financing NRW loss reduction programs can be a profitable venture. Since NRW is a problem faced worldwide, sukuk can provide the financing solution globally and venture into green financing.

References

Alavian et al. (2009). *World Bank water and climate change: Understanding the risks and making climate-smart investment decisions*. Washington, DC: World Bank.

American Society of Civil Engineers (ASCE). (2011). *Failure to act: The economic impact of current investment trends in water and wastewater treatment infrastructure*. http://www.asce.org/uploadedFiles/Issues_and_Advocacy/

Our_Initiatives/Infrastructure/Content_Pieces/failure-to-act-water-waste-water-report.pdf. Accessed July 2016.

Dighade, R. R., et al. (2015). Non revenue water reduction strategy in urban water supply system in India. *International Journal of Research in Engineering and Applied Sciences, 3*(1), 17–24.

Dobbs et al. (2013). *Infrastructure productivity: How to save $1 trillion a year.* New York: McKinsey Global Institute.

Faruqui, N. I., Biswas, A. K., & Bino, M. J. (2001). *Water management in Islam.* Ottawa: International Development Research Centre; Tokyo: United Nations University.

Frauendorfer, R., & Liemberger, R. (2010). *The issues and challenges of reducing non-revenue water.* Mandaluyong: Asian Development Bank.

Griffin, R. C., & Stoll, J. R. (1983). THE ENHANCED ROLE OF WATER CONSERVATION IN THE COST-BENEFIT ANALYSIS OF WATER PROJECTS. *JAWRA Journal of the American Water Resources Association, 19*(3), 447–457.

Hofwegen, P. V. (2006). *Financing water for all: Enhancing access to finance for local government, financing water for agriculture—Report of the gurria task force.* Marseille: World Water Council. Available at http://ww.worldwatercouncil.org.

Inman, M. (2010, September 29). 80 percent of global water supplies at risk. *National Geographic News.*

International Monetary Fund. (2015). *Issues in managing water challenges and policy instruments: Regional perspectives and case studies, technical companion notes.*

Kingdom et al. (2006, December). *The challenge of reducing Non-Revenue Water (NRW) in developing countries: How the private sector can help: A look at performance-based service contracting.* Water Supply and Sanitation Sector Board (Discussion Paper Series Paper No. 8), World Bank Group.

Levin, R. B., Epstein, P. R., et al. (2002). U.S. drinking water challenges in the twenty-first century. *Environmental Health Perspectives, 110,* 43–52.

Lloyd Owen, D. (2009). *Tapping liquidity: Financing water and wastewater to 2029, a report for PFI market intelligence.* London: Thomson Reuter.

Lobina et al. (2014). *Here to stay: Water remunicipalisation as a global trend.* Ferney-Voltaire: Public Services International Research Unit (PSIRU); Amsterdam: Transnational Institute (TNI).

London's water supply: A report by the London Assembly's Public Services Committee October 2003.

Malaysia Water Industry Guide (MWIG). (2015). Malaysian Water Association.

Marin et al. (2009). *Public-private partnerships for urban water utilities: A review of experiences in developing countries*. Washington, DC: The World Bank.

Moghul, U. F., & Safar-Aly, S. H. K. (2015). Green Sukuk: The introduction of Islam's environmental ethics to contemporary Islamic finance. *The Georgetown International Environmental Law Review, 27*, 1.

Moss et al. (2003, March). Valuing water for better governance—How to promote dialogue to balance social, environmental and economic values, CEO Panel Business and Industry, 10. March.

Neville Spykerman et al. (2016, April 16). Massive water crisis threatens nation. *The Star*. Saturday, http://www.thestar.com.my/news/nation/2016/04/16/massive-water-crisis-threatens-nation-water-levels-at-rivers-and-dams-dropping-acutely-by-the-day/. Accessed 11 July 2016.

OECD. (2007). *Infrastructure to 2030, volume 2, mapping policy for water, electricity and transport*. Paris: OECD.

OECD. (2009). *Private sector participation in water infrastructure*. Paris: OECD.

OECD. (2010). *Innovative finance mechanisms for the water sector*. Paris: OECD.

Rodriguez, D. J., van den Berg, C., & McMahon, A. (2012). *Investing in water infrastructure: Capital, operations, and maintenance* (Water papers). Washington, DC: The World Bank. http://documents.worldbank.org/curated/en/2012/11/17007405/investing-water-infrastructure-capital-operations-maintenance. Accessed 11 July 2016.

Sadoff, C. W., Hall, J. W., Grey, D., Aerts, J. C. J. H., Ait-Kadi, M., & Brown, C., et al. (2015). *Securing water, sustaining growth* (Report of the GWP/OECD Task Force on Water Security and Sustainable Growth), University of Oxford, UK, 180.

Shiklomanov, I. (1993). *World fresh water resources, water in crisis: A guide to the world's fresh water resources*. London: Oxford University Press.

Shoail, S., Shameem, J., Hussain, F. (2014). *Non-revenue water management in Pakistan*. Regional Workshop on "Capacity Development, Water Operators' Partnerships and Financing for Non-revenue Water Management" in Central Asian countries, 7–9 July, Dushanbe, Republic of Tajikistan.

Shore, D. G. (1988). Economic Optimization of Distribution Leakage Control. *Water and Environment Journal, 2*(5), 545–551.

The Global Risks 2015 Report, World Economic Forum.
The International Benchmarking Network for Water and Sanitation Utilities (IBNET).
Walski, T. M. (1984). *Analysis of Water Distribution Systems*, New York: Van Nostrand Reinhold Company.
Wasif, S. (2016, May 30). Pakistan may run dry by 2025: Study. *The Express Tribune Pakistan*, http://tribune.com.pk/story/1112704/pakistan-may-run-dry-2025-study/. Accessed 13 Aug 2016.
World Economic Forum (WEF). (2009). *Energy vision update 2009: Thirsty energy: Water in the 21st century, Geneva?* Englewood, CO: WEF/Cambridge Energy Research Associates. http://www.weforum.org/reports/thirsty-energy-water-and-energy-21st-century?fo=1. Accessed 11 July 2016.
Wickstrom, L. (2010). Islam and water: Islamic guiding principles on water management. *Managing blue gold: New perspectives on water security in the Levantine Middle East* (FIIA Report 25/2010).
Winpenny, J. (2003). *Financing water for all: Report of the world panel on financing water infrastructure.* World Water Council, Third World Water Forum and Global Water Partnership, Marseille, France (Camdessus Report 2003).
Winpenny et al. (2015). *Water: Fit to finance? Catalyzing national growth through investment in water security report of the high level panel on financing infrastructure for a water secure world*, April 2015. World Water Council and OECD.
World Bank. (2003). *Efficient, sustainable service for all? An OED review of the World Bank's assistance to water supply and sanitation.* Washington, DC: World Bank. http://documents.worldbank.org/curated/en/2003/09/2519895/efficient-sustainable-service-all-oed-review-world-banks-assistance-water-supply-sanitation. Accessed 11 July 2011.
World Bank. (2004a). *Water resources sector strategy: Strategic directions for World Bank engagement* (Vol. 1 of 1). http://wwwwds.worldbank.org/servlet/WDS_IBank_Servlet?pcont=details&eid=000090341_20040601150257. Accessed 11 July 2016.
World Bank. (2004b). *The World Bank group's program for water and sanitation.* http://siteresources.worldbank.org/INTWSS/Publications/20249484/WSS_report_Final_19Feb.pdf. Accessed 11 July 2016.
World Bank. (2004c). *Operational guidance for World Bank group staff: Public and private sector roles in water supply and sanitation services.* Washington, DC: Water Supply and Sanitation Sector Board. http://siteresources.

worldbank.org/INTWSS/Publications/20249486/Guidance%20note%20Public%20and%20Private%20Sector%20Roles%20in%20Water%20Supply%20and%20Sanitation%20Services%20Apr%2004.pdf. Accessed 11 July 2011.

World Bank Group. (2016). *High and dry: Climate change, water, and the economy*. Washington, DC: World Bank. © World Bank. https://openknowledge.worldbank.org/handle/10986/23665. License: CC BY 3.0 IGO.

Yeh, R. (2016). In pictures: Ground zero of Malaysia's water crisis. *Channel News Asia*. http://www.channelnewsasia.com/news/singapore/in-pictures-ground-zero/2748642.html. Accessed 11 July 2016.

Zetland, D. (2016). The struggle for residential water metering in England and Wales. *Water Alternatives, 9*(1), 120–138.

30 companies in Selangor suffer huge losses due to water crisis—Mahdzir-Bernama | November 10, 2014 14:06 MYT. http://english.astroawani.com/malaysia-news/30-companies-selangor-suffer-huge-losses-due-water-crisis-mahdzir-48080. Accessed 11 July 2016.

Role of Takaful in Raising Higher Education Enrollment in Pakistan

Muhammad Imran and Mohsin Khawja

Abstract This study analyzes how saving-based *Takaful* products can help people in Pakistan in planning the future for their children's education. We recorded feedback from a sample of 400 people belonging to the working class and have children under the age of 12 years. The survey assessed from them how they envision the education of their children. We find that saving-based *Takaful* products can help in providing children with a better and secure educational future. The views of the respondents clearly state the vitality of an investment plan which can be designed to provide adequate money for key educational milestones in a child's career. The study helps determine the fact that planning for children's education through *Shariah* -based products can help improve the overall enrollment rate in higher education in the country.

M. Imran (✉)
Institute of Business Administration, Karachi, Pakistan

M. Khawja
Center of Research Excellence for Islamic Banking & Finance,
Research Institute, King Fahd University of Petroleum and Minerals,
WWDhahran, Saudi Arabia

S.A.R. Rizvi and I. Saba (eds.), *Developments in Islamic Finance*, Palgrave CIBFR Studies in Islamic Finance, DOI 10.1007/978-3-319-59342-5_3

Keywords Takaful · Islamic insurance · BancaTakaful · Higher education · Pakistan

1 Introduction

Takaful[1] is a noun stemming from the Arabic verb "Kafal" which means guarantee or responsibility, or more generally "taking care of one's needs."

Thus, the word Takaful means shared responsibility, shared guarantee, collective assurance, and mutual undertakings. Islamic insurance acknowledges the concept of mutual protection and shared responsibility which was also seen under the Arab tribal custom in the practices of paying blood money (diyah). This was accepted into Islamic practice on the verdict of the Prophet (PBUH). It therefore portrays the sincerity and willingness of the group to help and assist anyone among them in times of need. "Takaful" possesses many similarities to co-operative or mutual insurance.

As mentioned in the Qur'an:

> "And help one another in righteousness and piety and do not help one another in evil deeds and enmity[2]

Takaful is based on shared responsibility, shared guarantee, collective assurance, and mutual undertakings. In Takaful, there are contributors instead of policyholders, who participate jointly in a fund for their mutual benefit. They are owners of the fund and the Takaful company manages the fund on their behalf. Thus, if the company makes a profit, this is shared between the contributors, and if any of the contributors were to suffer financial loss, they are paid from the Takaful fund.

Takaful can also be defined as… *a system based on solidarity pea e of mind and mutual protection which provides mutual financial and other forms of aid to Members {of the group} in case of specific need whereby Members mutually agree to contribute monies to support this common goal".*[3]

Takaful saving plan is also a good tool to enhance wealth as wealth plays an important role in human life. Wealth has always been a vital part of a human's life through which one can enjoy all the luxuries of life. Wealth is a subject matter of trade and any business dealings such as sales and leasing. Not importantly money but properties like houses, cars, or even lands are different forms of wealth which a person earns either through inheritance or of course by striving hard.[4] Allah (swt) has mentioned in the holy Quran "That man can have nothing but he strives for" (53:39).[5]

Normally, wealth planning comprises of five parts:

- Investment planning
- Tax planning
- Retirement planning
- Estate planning
- Education planning

Education plan is becoming more necessary as cost of education increases. There are benefits in tax and estate planning by properly planning for education. The earlier the start, the better it is for the education plan.[6]

There are several financial instruments that are acceptable in Shariah rules and principles for wealth management. Some are as follows:

- Deposits: examples are current accounts, savings accounts, and term deposits
- Investment
- Islamic mutual funds
- BancaTakaful

The Bank Insurance/Takaful Model ("BIM"), also sometimes known as "Bancassurance /Banca Takaful," is the term used to describe the partnership or relationship between a bank (conventional bank/Islamic bank) and an insurance company whereby the insurance company uses the bank sales channel in order to sell insurance/Takaful products.

BIM allows the insurance/Takaful company to maintain smaller direct sales teams as their products are sold through the bank-to-bank customers by bank staff. Bank staff and tellers, rather than an insurance/Takaful salesperson, become the point of sale/point of contact for the customer. Bank staff are advised and supported by the insurance/Takaful company through product information, marketing campaigns, and sales training.

Both the bank and insurance/Takaful company share the commission. Insurance policies are processed and administered by the insurance company. BIM differs from "Classic" or Traditional Insurance Model (TIM) in that TIM insurance companies tend to have larger insurance sales teams and generally work with brokers and third-party agents (Wikipedia).[7]

There are several needs in which product BancaTakaful can be helpful, for example:

- Wedding
- Life plan
- Education

This research focuses on what role can a bank play in increasing the education level at the tertiary level by bringing in education-based Takaful products in the market. This research focuses on the tertiary level as the cost of education at tertiary levels is high which means that the bank may come across sufficient funding need on individual basis.

Due to lack of resources, the researchers could conduct research on a random sample. More than three-fourth of the sample included respondents from a limited number of organizations; this resulted in a large majority of the respondents in the privately employed segment falling in the > 40,000 salary range. Most people in this salary range usually have considerable amount of monthly savings and explicitly or tacitly consider themselves to be secure when it comes to the education of their children. Thus, they do not as such find a need for education financing solutions.

There is a representation bias in the sample. Due to the sampling procedure adopted, the respondents cannot be used to represent the whole 30—to 35-year-old population. Almost all respondents in the privately employed category were well educated and highly paid, which is not true for a large part of the target population.

2 Research Methodology

For the research, a questionnaire has been designed keeping in mind the hypothesis and research objectives of the research. The questionnaire comprises of 25 questions, and research will be carried out in a one-on-one session as many questions are of subjective nature as well. The questionnaire will be tabulated, and responses will be analyzed to prove the hypothesis outlined in the section above.

The target market for the research includes the following:

- Male
- Adult
- Married, and with children who are less than 12.

The following research hypotheses will be proven to determine the need for education-based Takaful and savings products for funding tertiary education. For this purpose, researchers have tabulated and analyzed responses from 400 respondents which seek to provide answers to the following formulated hypotheses.

The reason for choosing this target market is that males normally make financial decisions in their families being the main breadwinner. Moreover, a married person who has children is more inclined to plan for his family's well-being as compared to a person who has no responsibilities whatsoever.

2.1 Research Hypothesis

1. People plan for their children's higher education.
    - This hypothesis aims to prove that people consider education as priority item among other expenditure and reserve their disposable income on periodic basis to save for their children's higher education expected in 10–15 years time.
2. If people had money, they would invest in long-term savings and Takaful plan to provide for their children's higher education.
    - This hypotheses aims to prove that non-availability of disposable funds is the reason people do not plan for their children's

education. People with disposable income will plan to provide higher education to their children.

3. Enrollment rate at postgraduate/university level will increase if people are provided with education-based banking products.
    - We seek to prove that there is a need as well as acceptance of education-based products to fund tertiary-level education. Moreover, there is a preference for Islamic-based education products as compared to conventional products.
4. People will prefer Takaful-based education products as compared to insurance-based education products.
    - We seek to prove that people of Pakistan hold on to their religious beliefs when given a choice between a Shariah compliant and a non-Shariah compliant products to satisfy their financial needs.

3 Literature Review

3.1 Present Scenario of Education System in Pakistan

Education plays a very vital role in the development of a country, and a direct correlation has been found between education level of a nation and its prosperity in terms of economic, social, and political well-being. Education raises the productivity and efficiency of individuals and thus produces skilled manpower that is capable of leading the economy toward the path of sustainable development. It is sad but true that the situation of the education sector in Pakistan is not very encouraging.[8] At this point, we will discuss some of the key indicators related to Pakistan's education sector. Please note that as the major studies used for literature review in this regard were conducted in 2009, the key indicators mentioned in the literature review are for the corresponding period as well.

3.1.1 Low Enrollment Rate

In addition to wide disparities between regions and gender, lack of trained teachers, deficiency of proper teaching materials, and poor

Table 1 GER%—comparison of South Asian Countries[1]

2007 GER%	Primary	Secondary	Tertiary
Pakistan	92	33	5
India	94	48	10
Bangladesh	91	43	7
Srilanka	109	86	–
Average	99.6	57.4	11.25

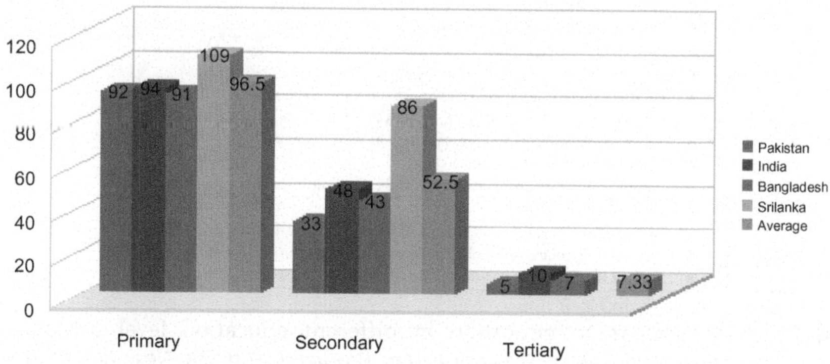

*India figures are of year 2002
[1]UNESCO UIS (institute of Statistics), *"Statistics In Brief For India, Sri Lanka, Bangladesh & Pakistan"*, 2007. (http://stats.uis.unesco.org/unesco)

physical infrastructure of schools, the most alarming situation in Pakistan is the drastic decrease in the enrollment level as one goes up the education level (Table 1).

As per the graph above, Pakistan has a gross enrollment rate of 92% at the primary level, which means that 92% of the pupils that are of the age that is represented by primary level are enrolled at primary level. This is the lowest as per the region's average of almost 100%. The enrollment rate drops drastically to 33% at secondary level and a mere 5% at tertiary level, which hints to a high dropout rate at secondary and tertiary levels. Enrollment rate of a mere 5% at tertiary level means that around 95% of the eligible population at tertiary level does not go to college or university. This low enrollment rate at tertiary level has resulted in non-availability of specialists in fields of medicine, engineering, and science and technology. There can be various reasons for such low enrollment rates at different levels of education as follows (Fig. 1):

Level	Possible Major Constraints[1]
Primary	• Lack of or poor perception of quality of education and utility of education. • Religious reservations about education in schools and focus on Quranic education • Focus on occupational skills learning rather than schooling • Presence of labor based occupations and lack of professional occupations • Control of landlords/power in few hands • Cultural constraints to let females study and they comprise of majority of population • Lack of and unwillingness of teachers to teach in rural, suburban areas • Lack of availability of schools due to funds constraints • Lack of Books and stationery • Lack of availability of transport services to reach schools • Funds available for basic needs only
Secondary	• Lack of or poor perception of quality of education and utility of education. • Lack of and unwillingness of teachers to teach in rural, suburban areas • Lack of availability of Middle level schools and colleges due to funds constraints • Lack of availability of transport services to reach schools • Too many dependents and pressure to work rather than study • Funds available for basic needs only • Presence of labor based occupations and lack of professional occupations
Tertiary	• Lack of universities • Lack of funds to relocate to urban areas where most of the universities are located • Too much of competition for seats in universities due to few universities • Lack of funds to afford graduate or postgraduate studies

Fig. 1 Major barriers to education at different education levels: [1]Memon, G.R. "*Education in Pakistan: The Key Issues, Problems and The New Challenges*" Department of Education, University of Karachi, Journal of Management and Social Sciences. 2007. Vol. 3, No. 1

3.1.2 Government Spending on Education

Like other social sectors, education is not a priority area of the Pakistani government as is represented by the low percentage of education spending to the GDP of Pakistan. The spending on education has actually dropped from 1.86% to 1.74% in the fiscal year 2007–2008 (Fig. 2).

Britain's £77 million expenditure for the year 2007–2008 was about 6% of its GDP and exceeded by more than twice the £32 billion assigned to the defense of this once mighty world power. Japan, the second largest world economy, also spends about 10% of its national budget for education-related facilities and has a 9-year system of compulsory education. Last year, about 242 billion was awarded as an operating capital to its 93 universities to revitalize their creativity in international competition (Table 2).

The percentage of GDP given to education by some other vibrant industrial economies such as 5.91% by Australia, 6.285 by Canada, 7.38%

The 1973 constitution of the Islamic Republic of Pakistan recognizes the importance of education and says that the state shall:

(i) Promote unity and observance of the Islamic moral standards;
(ii) Promote with special care the educational and economic interests of backward areas;
(iii) Remove illiteracy and provide free and compulsory secondary education within minimum possible period;
(iv) Make technical and professional education generally available and higher education equally accessible to all on the basis of merit;
(v) Enable the people of different areas, through education, training, agriculture and industrial development, and other methods to participate fully in all form of national activities including employment in the services of Pakistan; and
(vi) Ensure full participation of women in all the spheres of national life

Fig. 2 Clause on Education in Islamic Constitution of Pakistan[1]. Akram, M. & Khan, F. J. "*Public provision of Education and Government spending in Pakistan*", Pakistan Institute of Development Economics (PIDE). 2007. Working paper 40

Table 2 Government spending on education as % of GDP[1]

Year	2001–2002	2002–2003	2003–2004	2004–2005	2005–2006	2006–2007	2007–2008
Spending %	1.51	1.63	1.73	1.78	1.86	1.86	1.74

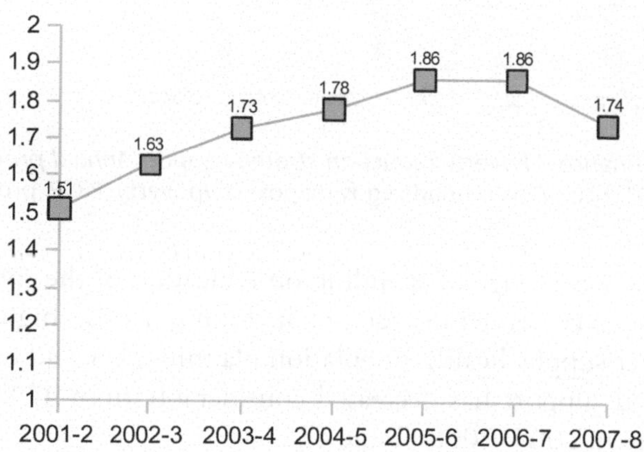

[1]Ministry of Finance, "Poverty Reduction Strategy Paper: Annual Progress Report FY 2007–2008". http://www.finance.gov.pk/poverty/poverty_PRSP_progress.aspx

by Denmark, and 6.01% by France is also illustrative. These inputs, interestingly, do not include the expenditure incurred on research, training, and development in other manufacturing and technological sectors[9] (Table 3).

Education has always been the biggest receiver of spending from the PRSP (poverty reduction strategy paper–pro-poor expenditure).

Table 3 Spending on education vs total spending[1]

Year	2001–2002	2002–2003	2003–2004	2004–2005	2005–2006	2006–2007	2007–2008
Spending on education	66290	78,447	97,697	116,873	141,702	162,084	182,646
Total spending	166,074	209,043	209,043	316,243	376,139	426,680	572,620
% of spending	40%	38%	47%	37%	38%	38%	32%

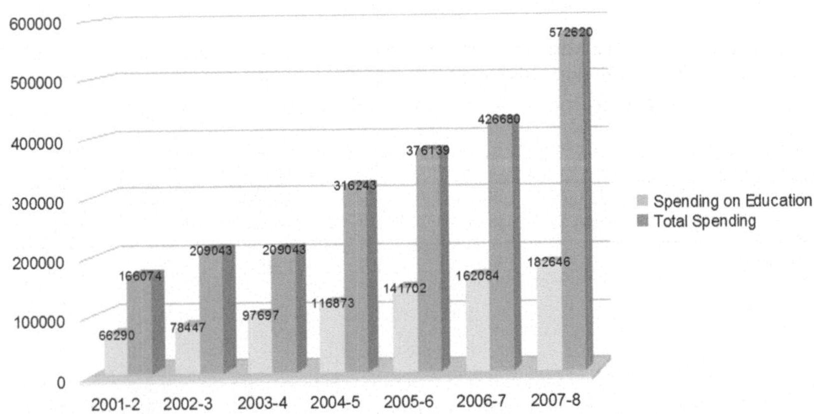

[11]Ministry of finance, "*Poverty reduction strategy paper: Annual progress report FY 2007–2008*". http://www.finance.gov.pk/poverty/poverty_PRSP_progress.aspx

However, the percentage of spending on education of the total amount spent on poverty reduction factors including roads, highways, and bridges, water supply, health, population planning, law and order, housing, and food support has decreased considerably from 47% in 2003–2004 to 32% in 2007–2008 (Table 4).

As per the graph above, education spending at tertiary level, i.e., college/universities/professional and technical universities has increased considerably from 2001–2002 to 2007–2008. However, the enrollment rate at tertiary level in Pakistan is still the lowest in the region. The government has renewed its focus from primary- to tertiary-level education over time, and it is a matter of time when we will see considerable conversion of primary and secondary students making their way up the education level.

Table 4 % of education spending on different levels of education[1]

Year	2001–2002	2002–2003	2003–2004	2004–2005	2005–2006	2006–2007	2007–2008
Primary education	47.23	42.4	44.32	42.18	37.99	32.53	27.79
Secondary education	25.21	25.81	24	23.46	23.89	21.23	18.19
General university/ college education	12.15	16.19	15.27	12.31	20.62	22.32	20.65
Professional/technical universities	5.67	5.08	4.86	11	5.84	4.54	4.8
Teacher and vocational training	4.54	2.18	1.88	1.97	1.62	1.97	0.24
Other educational institutions	5.21	8.33	9.66	9.09	10.03	17.41	12.55

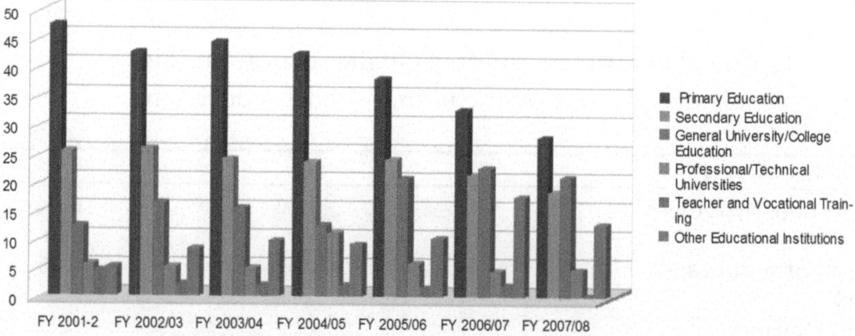

[1]Ministry of finance, "*Poverty reduction strategy paper: Annual progress report FY 2007–2008*". http://www.finance.gov.pk/poverty/poverty_PRSP_progress.aspx

Currently, the government bailout package from the IMF of $7.6 billion has resulted in increased pressure on the developmental spending on education as the government has committed to the International Monetary Fund (IMF) to reduce the fiscal deficit from 7.4% of GDP in 2007–2008 financial year to 4.2% in the current fiscal year.[10] The government has actually taken the following actions directly affecting the education sector:

- Education sector has faced cuts of Rs. 30 billion out of the total Rs. 79.5 billion proposed cuts in PSDP allocation to reduce fiscal deficit.
- Funding for the higher education sector has been cut by 73%. Officials have attributed lack of cash and economic slowdown for the huge cut. The government will now spend only Rs. 114 billion, instead of the previously allocated Rs. 412 billion for executing 600 projects.

- Government has directed the HEC to abolish a project worth Rs. 160 billion under which four new engineering universities were to be set up in the country.
- The science and technology subsector appears to be the hardest hit; its funding will be reduced by Rs. 10.6 billion.
- Deep cuts have also been made for the information and communication technology subsector; it will get Rs. 34.9 billion less than the allocated Rs. 60 billion for executing 118 projects.[11]

Hypothesis Testing

Hypothesis # 1: People plan for their children's higher education

Ho: People plan for their children's higher education (Fig. 3).
H1: People not plan for their children's higher education.

Null hypothesis	p	=	63%
Alternate hypothesis	p0	=	60%
	n	=	400
Level of significance			0.05
Tail		=	2
Test statistics	$z = \frac{\hat{p} - p_0}{\sqrt{\frac{p_0(1-p_0)}{n}}}$		
Calculated value		=	1.225
Tabulated value		=	−1.96
Decision			Accept

Level of significance: 95% confidence interval

For our calculation, we have assumed that at least 60% of our sample should plan for their children's higher education, otherwise it would be assumed that the people living in Pakistan are not planning of their children's higher education.

Since the calculated value falls in the acceptance region, at the 5% significance level, we do not have enough data to reject the hypothesis that people plan for their children's higher education. Therefore, we will accept the hypothesis.

Hypothesis Testing # 2: If people had money, they would invest in long-term savings and Takaful plan to provide for their children's higher education.

	Frequency	%
Yes	252	63.00%
No	148	37.00%
Total	400	

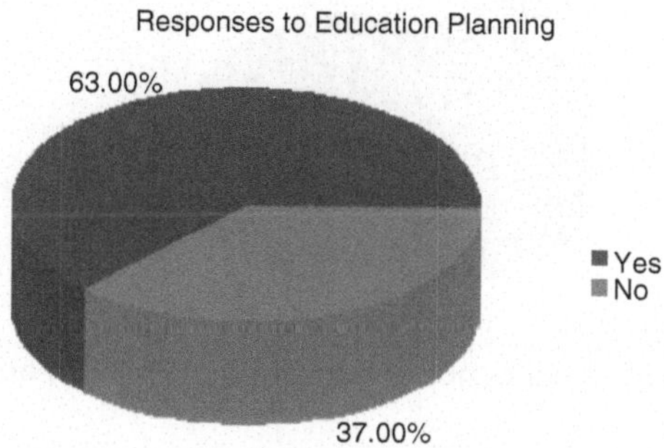

Fig. 3 Distribution of responses to education planning of sample

Ho: If people had money, they would invest in long-term savings and Takaful plan to provide for their children's higher education-Higher education.

H1: If people had money, still they would not invest in long-term savings and Takaful plan to provide for their children's higher education (Fig. 4).

Null hypothesis	p	=	64%
Alternate hypothesis	p0	=	60%
	n	=	400
Level of significance			0.05
Tail		=	2
Test statistics	$z = \frac{\hat{p} - p_0}{\sqrt{\frac{p_0(1-p_0)}{n}}}$		
Calculated value		=	1.633
Tabulated value		=	−1.96
Decision			Accept

Level of significance: 95% confidence interval

For our calculation, we have assumed that at least 60% of our sample invest money for their children's higher education, otherwise it would be assumed that the people living in Pakistan are not investing in long-term savings and Takaful plan.

Yes	255	63.75%
No	143	35.75%
	400	

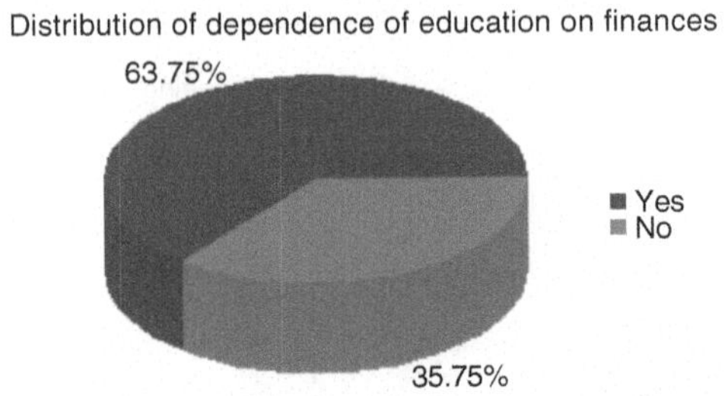

Fig. 4 Distribution of dependence of education of children on finances

Since the calculated value falls in the acceptance region, at the 5% significance level, we do not have enough data to reject that if people had money, they would invest in long-term savings and Takaful plan to provide their children's higher education. Therefore, we will accept the hypothesis.

Hypothesis # 3: Enrollment rate at Postgraduate/university level will increase if people are provided with education-based banking products (Figs. 5, 6).

We have already proven that the low enrollment rate at graduate and postgraduate education is also due to lack of finances to fund education costs. We can therefore presume that if people avail education-based products, then the funding gap can be reduced to an extent that the enrollment can be increased at the graduate and postgraduate levels. As per our primary research, 68% of respondents felt that they will be having the necessary funds to provide for their children's education, while around 32% felt they would not be having them.

Out of these 32% respondents, an astounding 94.57% of the people who had not planned for their children's education said they will be interested in a banking solution to help them arrange funds for their children's graduate and postgraduate education.

Hypothesis # 4: People will prefer Takaful -based education products as compared to insurance-based education products.

Yes	271	67.75%
No	129	32.25%
	400	

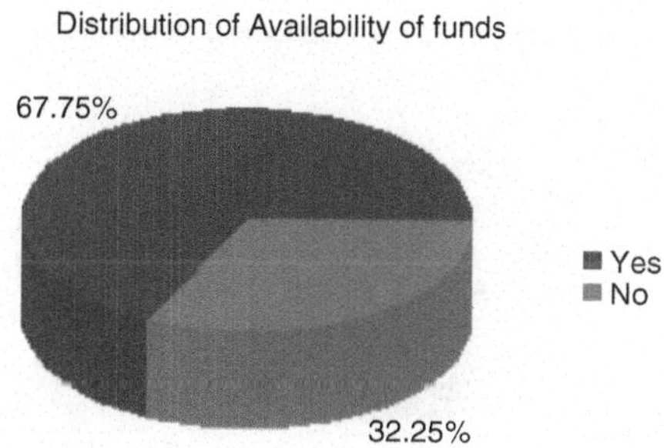

Fig. 5 Distribution of availability of funds

	Frequency%	
No	7	5.43%
Yes	122	94.57%
Total	129	

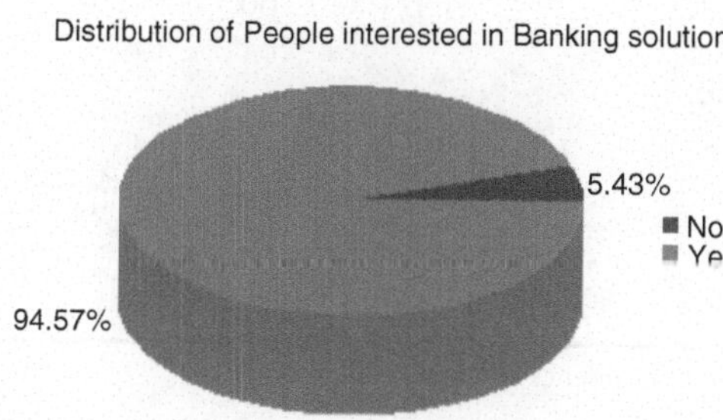

Fig. 6 Distribution of people investment options availed by sample

We seek to prove that people of Pakistan hold on to their religious beliefs when given a choice between a Shariah compliant and a non-Shariah compliant products to satisfy their financial needs.

Ho: People will prefer Takaful-based education products as compared to insurance-based education products.

Yes	332	83.00%
No	68	17.00%
	400	

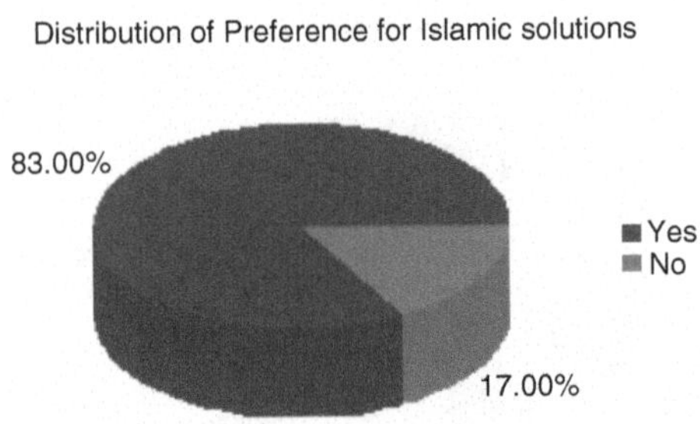

Fig. 7 Distribution of preference for Islamic solutions

H1: People will not prefer Takaful-based education products as compared to insurance-based education products (Fig. 7).

Null hypothesis	p	=	83%
Alternate hypothesis	p0	=	85%
	n	=	400
Level of significance			0.05
Tail		=	2
Test statistics	$z = \frac{\hat{p} - p_0}{\sqrt{\frac{p_0(1-p_0)}{n}}}$		
Calculated value		=	−1.120
Tabulated value		=	−1.96
Decision			Accept

Level of significance: 95% confidence interval

For our calculation, we have assumed that at least 85% of our sample will prefer Takaful -based education products as compared to insurance-based education products, otherwise it would be assumed that the people living in Pakistan will not prefer Takaful -based education products as compared to insurance-based education products.

Since the calculated value falls in the acceptance region, at the 5% significance level, we do not have enough data to reject that people will prefer Takaful-based education products as compared to insurance-based education products. Therefore, we will accept the hypothesis.

4 Conclusions

From the above results, we conclude as follows:

- People do plan for their children's education. Individual with many children and with disposable income has the tendency to plan ahead for their children's education.
- People of lower-income groups consider their decision to educate their children at higher levels depending on the availability of funds. Moreover, people in higher-income brackets and hence with higher disposable income can spare more funds to invest in savings plan to provide for the future education needs of their children.
- People of low-income group consider availability of finances as one of the major factors in their decision to send their children for higher education.
- People who are not prepared to finance their children's education will avail education-based products if provided which will increase the enrollment at graduate and postgraduate education in return.
- People who had previous investment avenues will also look into the possibility of investing in Takaful and savings product as most of the other modes of investment do not protect against financial insecurity due to untimely death of respondents.
- People of Pakistan are driven by their religious beliefs while making financial decisions, and given a choice, they will always prefer Islamic products over conventional ones.

5 Recommendation

Since the formation of Higher Education Commission (HEC), a large number of postgraduate students benefited by the donations provided to them by HEC to pursue their higher education. However, since the year 2008, the economic downturn in Pakistan has created a negative impact on the funding of HEC by the government, which in turn dried down the funding by HEC to students to pursue higher education.

Keeping in view the present economic scenario and the findings of this research, it is recommended that the government should arrange awareness program for promotion of Takaful -based saving products at mass level. This will help the people realize about a new avenue of savings through which they can utilize their own savings to fund for their children's higher education. The government should also take an initiative to include Takaful-based saving plans as an incentive for its employees so that they can help their children get best of education in future. These steps can also be taken by the private sector organizations. In this manner, there will be more awareness among the citizens regarding savings-based Takaful product; as a result, the people of Pakistan will be able to plan for their children's higher education in a proactive and Shariah compliant way.

Notes

1. Asmatullah, "*Takaful kee Sharai Haisyat*", Idaratul Ma'arif Karachi, 2009. P. 72 (Asmatullah 2009).
2. Al Quran, Surah-Al-Maida: (5:2).
3. Fisher, O. "*Takaful Markets & products*", A Training Reference Manual, Unicorn Investment Bank, Bahrain. 2008 (Fisher 2008).
4. Billah, M. M. "*Islamic Wealth Management & World View". 2008. p 1.* www.takaful.coop/doc_store/takaful/WealthMgt.doc (Billah 2008).
5. Al Quran, Surah-Al-Najm: (53:39).
6. Abdul Razak, S. H. "*Wealth Planning and Management". 2007.*
7. http://en.wikipedia.org/wiki/Bancassurance.
8. Akram, M. and Khan, F. J. "*Public provision of Education and Government spending in Pakistan*", Pakistan Institute of Development Economics (PIDE). 2007. Working paper 40 (Akram and Khan 2007).
9. Habib, S. "*Imperatives of increased investment in education*". 2009.
10. Shafique, K. "*Budget Cuts for Higher Education: A Sad State of Affairs*", STEP(Science, technology and Education in Pakistan). 2009. http://www.nextstepforward.net (Shafique 2009).
11. Khan,S.B. "*Higher education spending cut by 73 percent*". 2009.

Appendix

Appendix:

QUESTIONNAIRE FOR PRIMARY RESEARCH

1. Name : __________
2. Age : __________
3. Address. ____________
4. Monthly Income :
   < 20 K ☐ < 30 K ☐ < 40 K ☐< 50 K ☐More than 50 K ☐
5. Gender : Male☐ Female☐
6. Occupation : Self Employed ☐ Salaried ☐
7. How many Children do you have?
   One☐ Two☐ Three☐ More☐
8. How old are your Children?

	Gender	0-3	4-7	7-10	10-13	13 & above
1st Child						
2nd Child						
3rd Child						

9. Have you planned for your children's education? Yes☐ No☐
10. Do you have daughters? Yes☐ No☐ How many _________
11. If yes, How much do you plan to educate your daughters?
    Primary ☐ Secondary ☐ Graduate☐ Post Graduate ☐
12. Do you think it is equally important to educate your daughters? Yes☐ No☐
13. How much do you plan to educate your sons?
    Primary ☐ Secondary ☐ Graduate ☐ Post Graduate☐

14. Is the decision to educate your children dependent on availability of funds?

    Yes ☐ No ☐

15. If you plan to educate your sons more than your daughters, is this decision based on lack of finances? Yes ☐ No ☐

16. How much funds do you think you need to provide graduate/postgraduate education to your children?

    < 5 Lacs ☐ < 15 Lacs ☐ < 25 Lacs ☐ < 40 Lacs ☐ < 50 Lacs ☐ More ☐

17. Do you think you will have funds to provide graduate/postgraduate education to your children? Yes ☐ No ☐

    If Yes, How do you plan to arrange for such funds? Tick as many as applicable

    ☐ Monthly savings

    ☐ Investment in real estate

    ☐ Investment in stocks

    ☐ Investment in insurance policy

    ☐ Investment in government saving schemes-NSS/DSS

    ☐ Loan

18. If No, will you be interested in a solution that will help you arrange funds for your children's graduate/post graduate education?

    Yes ☐ No ☐

19. Are your children secure in case you suffer an untimely death or disability that restricts you from earning?

    Yes ☐ No ☐

20. If Yes, How have you secured them?

    ☐ Monthly savings

    ☐ Investment in real estate

    ☐ Investment in stocks

    ☐ Investment in Insurance policy

    ☐ Investment in government saving schemes-NSS/DSS

21. If No, will you be interested in a solution that will help you arrange funds for your children's graduate/post graduate education in case you are not there to provide for them?

    Yes ☐ No ☐

22. Are you aware of any savings/insurance products focused on your child/s education?

    Yes ☐ No ☐ if Yes, please state ______________________________

23. Given a choice, would you prefer Islamic insurance plans over conventional insurance plans? Yes☐ No ☐

References

Akram, M. & Khan, F. J. (2007). *Public provision of education and government spending in Pakistan* (Working Paper No. 40). Islamabad: Pakistan Institute of Development Economics (PIDE).

Asmatullah. (2009). *Takaful kee Sharai Haisyat*. Karachi: Idaratul Ma'arif.

Billah, M. M. (2008). *Islamic wealth management & world view.* www.takaful.coop/doc_store/takaful/WealthMgt.doc.

Fisher, O. (2008). *Takaful markets & products. A training reference manual.* Bahrain: Unicorn Investment Bank.

Shafique, K. (2009). *Budget cuts for higher education: A sad state of affairs, STEP (Science, technology and Education in Pakistan).* http://www.nextstepforward.net.

Ṣukūk Default and Issues in Their Resolution: The Case of Villamar Ṣukūk

Salman Syed Ali

Abstract Several high-profile *Sukuk* have defaulted in recent years. The phenomenon has created upheaval in the *sukuk* market and affected its development and investors' confidence. Smooth resolution of default and bankruptcy is quite important for the financial instruments and their markets. The purpose of this study is to understand the nature and causes of the difficulties encountered in quick settlement of defaulted *sukuk*. It also aims to identify the Shariah issues faced in the resolution and settlement processes. Specifically, we focus on Villamar *Sukuk*. It was a *Musharakah sukuk* launched in 2008, after the issuance of the 2007 AAOIFI revised Shariah standard for *sukuk*. The Villamar *sukuk* was

I am thankful to an anonymous referee for evaluation and helpful comments on an earlier version. I also thank the participants of seminars at IRTI, Jeddah, 2016; International Islamic University, Islamabad, 2016; World Islamic Finance Forum 2016, Karachi; and IIFM Forum at WIBC 2016, Bahrain, for their comments and discussions which helped me to remove some factual errors and improved the exposition of the issues. All remaining errors are mine.

S.S. Ali (✉)
Islamic Research and Training Institute (IRTI), IDB,
Jeddah, Saudi Arabia
e-mail: ssyedali@isdb.org

S.A.R. Rizvi and I. Saba (eds.), *Developments in Islamic Finance*, Palgrave CIBFR Studies in Islamic Finance, DOI 10.1007/978-3-319-59342-5_4

unique in that it was a *Musharakah sukuk* without the buyback promise, thus complying with this aspect of the AAOIFI's revised *sukuk* standard. The paper analyzes the following: How a *Musharakah sukuk* can ever default? What operational and structuring factors cause delay in default resolution of a *Musharakah sukuk*? The paper derives several lessons from this episode and proposes regulatory and governance measures that can improve resolution of *sukuk* default and expedite their settlement.

Keywords *Sukuk* · Default · Insolvency · *Musharakah sukuk* · Shariah compliance

JEL Classification G10 · G33

1 Introduction

While many innovations are taking place in the *sukuk* structures that are indeed favorable for the development of Islamic capital markets, the requirements for their offerings and management to maturity also pose new institutional, governance, and regulatory challenges.[1] Several high-profile *Sukuk* have defaulted in recent years. The phenomenon has created upheaval in the *sukuk* market and affected its development and investors' confidence. While defaults are not unfamiliar for *sukuk* or for any other financial instrument, smooth resolution of default and bankruptcy is quite important for the financial instruments and their markets. In the absence of a quick and foreseeable resolution method, the confidence of the market is affected. Delayed and uncertain settlement of defaulted *sukuk* signifies weak institutional setup and poor governance that can hinder the development of Islamic capital markets.

Despite the difficulties faced by the Islamic finance industry in handling and resolving defaulted *sukuk*, not much has been done so far on creating default resolution regimes for *sukuk* at the regulatory level. A gap also exists on the theoretical side, as there is no significant body of literature on resolution of *sukuk* default. The only exception in the regulatory sphere is a general Shariah standard on default, issued by AAOIFI); however, it does not address many specific issues faced by the *sukuk* in default. In the legal and economics literature, few papers [e.g., Salah (2010), and Van Wijnbergen and Zaheer (2013)] describe and document the default of some high-profile *sukuk*, but do not address the resolution mechanisms and their difficulties.

The prohibition of interest by Shariah and its general emphasis on transparency, truthfulness, and fairness in dealings should have made resolution of a default or bankruptcy quick and smooth. However, the reality in the *sukuk* market is that it takes a very long time and complex negotiations to settle a default or a bankruptcy. While there is much talk in the news and in court filings, not much is known on the kind of difficulties faced in practical terms in re-negotiating and re-structuring of *sukuk*. It is not clear whether the *sukuk* prospectuses and other documents anticipate default and incorporate default resolution clauses in the issuance documents.

2 The Purpose

The purpose of this study is to understand the nature and causes of the difficulties encountered in quick settlement of defaulted *sukuk*. It also aims to identify the Shariah issues faced in the resolution and settlement processes. Since we know that the nature of the problems encountered in the default resolution will greatly depend on the type of *sukuk* under consideration, therefore, to keep this case study within practicable boundaries, we focus attention on *Musharakah sukuk* only. Specifically, we focus on Villamar *Sukuk*. It was a *Musharakah sukuk* launched in 2008, after the issuance of the 2007 AAOIFI revised Shariah standard for *sukuk*. The revised standard was issued in response to the controversy over the legitimacy of many *sukuk* products, particularly the *Musharakah sukuk* in which the capital of a partner is guaranteed by a buyback promise by the other partner. The Villamar *Sukuk* was unique in that it was a *Musharakah sukuk* without the buyback promise, thus complying with this aspect of the AAOIFI's revised *sukuk* standard. We analyze this *sukuk* and its default with a view to finding:

1. How a *Musharakah sukuk* can ever default?
2. What operational and structuring factors cause delay in default resolution of *Musharakah sukuk*?
3. What lessons can be learned from this episode?

3 The Scene

While the issuance of international *sukuk* has steadily increased from its debut in 2001–2014 with some decline in 2009 and 2010, the cumulative value of total issuance during this period has reached to US$91.77 billion. Combined with the growth, the variety in the *sukuk* structures has also increased from the initially issued basic Ijarah *sukuk* to many new structures, including the *sukuk* based on *Musharakah* (partnership). However, default on international *sukuk* has also increased particularly after the global financial crisis. So far ten high-profile *sukuk* have defaulted. Among these, 3 are in Bahrain, 2 in Kuwait, 1 in Saudi Arabia, 3 in UAE, and 1 in USA (See Table 1). However, technically, the Nakheel Group *Sukuk* did not default as the financially distressed *sukuk* was promised for bailout at the last moment by the government of UAE. Setting aside this one case, the nine *sukuk* in default amounted to US$3.166 billion and accounted for about 7% of the total *sukuk* issuance by 2008.

Table 1 The ten *Ṣukūk* in default after the global financial crisis

The Nakheel Group—UAE	International Investment Corporation—Kuwait
Gulf Holding Company (Villamar *Ṣukūk*)—Bahrain	Saad Group (Golden Belt)—Saudi Arabia
Dana Gas—UAE	Arcapita Bank—Bahrain
Gulf Finance House—Bahrain	The Investment Dar—Kuwait
Tabreed *Ṣukūk*—UAE	East Cameron Partners—USA

4 Case of Villamar *Sukuk*

The Villamar *Sukuk* offered in 2008 targeted to mobilize US$190 million to mature in 2013 (5-year maturity) for the development of a real estate project. It was characterized as a "*MusharakahSukuk*" in which the issuer (Villamar *Sukuk* Company Limited) and the originator (a single-person vehicle, Residential South Real Estate Development Co. (RSRED)) formed a partnership (*Musharakah*) to develop and construct three multistory-buildings complexes and sell the residential units to third parties. Profits obtained were to be distributed between the issuer and the originator according to a pre-agreed ratio. The issuer, being a trustee and representative of *sukuk* holders, would then distribute its share of the profit to the *Sukuk* holders. In case of losses, these were to be distributed between the issuer and the originator according to their respective contributions in the capital of the project. The issuer's portion of the losses subsequently was to pass to the *sukuk* holders. The business model of the construction project was such that in addition to the *sukuk* process, it relied on off-sale of the residential units to generate funds for the construction and completion of the project.

Unfortunately, the real estate development project ran into problems in 2010 in the aftermath of the global financial crisis when the demand for residential and commercial units weakened such that the off-sales were even weaker. Hence, the Villamar *Sukuk* that was floated for funding the project also runs into difficulties within 2 years of its issuance. It was reported in the finance industry that the project company was facing cash constraints,[2] news that the company tried to deny.[3] The liquidity crunch was real, though, resulting in *sukuk* default. Court cases were filed, negotiations took place, and the resolution of the *sukuk* is continuing to this date. Recently it has been announced that Al-Rajhi Bank and other parties are coming together to revive the project once again.[4] Even after 5 years since the default, resolution is still not completed; the recent deal merely pushed the debt problem forward for another 6 years.[5]

Before we proceed to discuss the difficulties that this *sukuk* encountered and why its resolution and restructuring are slow, it is important

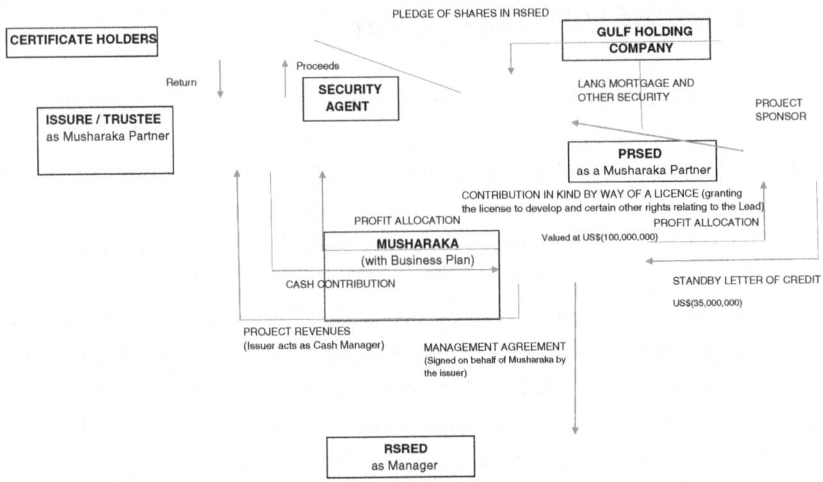

Fig. 1 Sukuk structure

to understand the structure of Villamar *Sukuk*, the key parties involved, and their mutual relationships. We will see that majority of the problems in *sukuk* resolution stem from deficiencies in the *sukuk* structure and the conflict of interests built into it to float it as a lookalike of a partnership, although it was essentially a debt contract with fixed obligations toward the *sukuk* holders.

5 Structure of Villamar *Sukuk*

The following Fig. 1 summarizes the structure of the *sukuk,* and the section below, it describes the key parties and their roles in this structure.

6 Key Parties to the Structure of the *Sukuk*, Their Roles, and the Underlying Main Assets

The **issuer** (Villamar *Sukuk* Company Limited) issued *Sukuk* to mobilize funds (US$190 million). The issuer was an exempted limited liability company incorporated in the Cayman Islands having a share capital of US$250 consisting of 250 shares with a nominal value of US$1 each. These shares were fully paid and held by Walkers SPV Limited as trustee of the Villamar *Sukuk* Company Limited Share Trust. The issuer also served as a trustee of the *Sukuk* holders.

The **originator** of this deal was Residential South Real Estate Development Co. ("**RSRED**"), a single-person company incorporated in the Kingdom of Bahrain on December 28, 2005. RSRED had a paid up share capital of BD 37,502,880, and it was 100% owned by Gulf Holding Company (GHC). The Gulf Holding Company ("**GHC**"), a Kuwaiti shareholding company incorporated in the State of Kuwait in 2005 with a total paid-up capital of KD70 million (approximately US$243 million), was the sponsor of the project.

The funds thus mobilized through *sukuk* were then invested in a ***Musharakah*** formed between the Villamar *Sukuk* Company Limited (issuer) and the Residential South Real Estate Development Co. ("RSRED"). Specifically, the *Musharakah* was created by the two *Musharakah* partners: (1) RSRED and (2) the issuer (Villamar *Sukuk* Company Limited). The partner 2 (*sukuk* issuer) contributed the *sukuk* proceeds (US$190 million) to the *Musharakah* capital, while the partner 1 (RSRED) contributed in-kind capital only: (a) granting of a license to construct on the land (internally valued at US$100 million)[6] and (b) a standby letter of credit (US$35 million). The *Musharakah* was to develop and construct three multistory-buildings complexes and sell the residential units to third parties.

The issuer as a partner in the *Musharakah* also acted as **Cash Manager** for the *Musharakah*. The Cash Manager was to operate accounts and calculate the distributable profits of the *Musharakah* (if any) and distribute to the *Musharakah* partners in the agreed *Musharakah* profit allocations annually till the winding up of the *Musharakah* (expected after 5 years from the issuance of *Sukuk*). The other partner in the *Musharakah* (i.e., RSRED) was made the **Manager** of the project. In this capacity, it was appointed as an independent contractor by each of the *Musharakah* Partners to provide certain services to the *Musharakah*, including (among other things) procuring the completion and delivery of the project.

The link between the *Sukuk* holders and the construction project was made remote (or indirect) by creation of a **trust** with the issuer appointed as **trustee** to hold assets in trust on behalf of the *Sukuk* holders. The **trust assets** mainly consisted of the issuer's undivided beneficial share in the *Musharakah* Assets, the *Sukuk* holders' rights, and entitlements under the Security Package, and other rights and receivables of the issuer.

With this structure, each ***Sukuk*** certificate evidenced an undivided beneficial ownership in the trust assets calculated *pro rata* based on the face value of the *Sukuk* certificates and ranked *pari passu*, without any preference, with the other *Sukuk* certificates.

7 Analysis

7.1 Can a Musharakah Default?

The scenario that a *Musharakah sukuk* has defaulted is itself surprising. How can a *Musharakah sukuk* default? By definition, default means breaching some obligation of payment. A default can occur in a debt contract when the borrower is unable to pay a contractual amount of the obligation in time, e.g., the interest installment during the period of the contract or the debt principal amount at the end. In a *Musharakah*, the partners share in profits and losses, so there is no contractually defined fixed payment. Hence, there can never be default in *Musharakah,* but a bankruptcy or insolvency is possible if the business is not continued due to low levels of profit. The winding up is a matter of selling the assets and distributing the proceeds among the partners pro rata to their respective share capital in the business.

However, the financial problems in continuation of the real estate project leading to no payments to the *sukuk* holders were labeled as default in Villamar *Sukuk* and restructuring as bankruptcy proceedings and litigations got underway.

The reason for this anomaly can be seen in the structure of the Villamar *Sukuk* which was essentially a pure debt secured by a mortgage and a standby letter of credit, but portrayed as a *Musharakah*. The actual *Musharakah* that was created between the issuer and RSRED had nothing to do with the *sukuk* holders; they were made one step remote from the *Musharakah* through interposition of the trust between *sukuk* holders and the project. Further, that *Musharakah* was also fictional in the sense that one partner (RSRED) was given full control of the project and a special treatment of granting a fixed fee for its services. Moreover, the *Musharakah* asset itself was mortgaged with a security agent.

The incentive payment structure was also strange in that the *sukuk* holders would receive LIBOR plus a margin, whereas the other partner RSRED would receive the rest of the amount. It is important to note that in the Villamar *sukuk* payment to *sukuk* holders has no sensitivity (or variation) with the actual performance of the *Musharakah*; the only connection is triggered when there is a very significant bad performance leading to discontinuation of the project.

7.2 What Are the Key Features of a Musharakah and Test of Its Validity?

The difference between an interest-based debt contract and a partnership contract lies in the conflict of interests and alignment of interests of the two parties. In interest-bearing debt, if a default occurs, then the interests of the lender diverge greatly from that of the borrower. The lender would like to get the interest payment as well as whatever amount of the principal is recoverable, even if this move leaves nothing for the borrower.

In case of partnership, if a loss occurs it will be shared pro-rata in proportion of the capital share of the partners. If they decide to continue the business with diminished amount of capital, they can carry on. If they decide to close the business, they can do it and share the residual value in the same proportion as their capital share. If one partner wants to continue the business while other wants to close, the one who wants to continue can buy the share of the exiting partner and acquire the business or he can invite new partner(s). In short, the interests of the two parties move in harmony both during the upside and during the downside of the business in a partnership contract. However, this is not true in case of interest-based debt contract.

When we examine the payment structure of the two parties in Villamar *sukuk,* we find that the issuer agreed to receive an amount fixed with no relation to project's performance. That is, issuer's reward was equal to the LIBOR plus a margin together multiplied by his contributed principal amount multiplied by the number of days it is invested out of 360 days of the year. Any extra mount of profit over and above this was allocated as the share of the RSRED as incentive payment. This, itself, is very unlikely reward profile for a partner who would expose his capital to business risk. However, a third party cannot legally challenge it easily because in a *Musharakah,* the profit sharing arrangement is up to the mutual agreement of the partners.[7]

However, in case of loss, the same freedom of mutually agreed loss bearing is not allowed. A quick test of whether a partnership (*Musharakah*) contractual structure is Shariah compliant is in examining how it handles situations of bankruptcy and dissolution of the *Musharakah*. Key characteristic of a Shariah-compliant *Musharakah* is that *the partners get, after settling any outstanding debts and costs, the residual amount of the asset in proportion to their respective shares in the capital.*

The *sukuk* offering document states that the losses would be shared in proportion to the outstanding capital of the respective partners. However, by use of several legal tricks, it was ensured that the losses were not shared in the above-stated manner. The first trick was to add a Security Package (mortgage and a standing letter of credit) to support the payment of the above-stated LIBOR plus margin and the principal amount to the *Sukuk* holders. This is similar to providing a financial guarantee[8] by one partner to the other partner, an arrangement that is not allowed in a *Musharakah.*

The second trick was the sequencing of payments. The *Sukuk* holders were to be "redeemed in full prior to the Scheduled Dissolution Date upon the occurrence of a Dissolution Event." Moreover, "[e]ach *Sukuk* Certificate will be redeemed at the aggregate principal amount of such *Sukuk* Certificate then outstanding plus any accrued and unpaid Periodic Distribution Amounts as at such date" (see page 26 of the offering circular). This clearly shows its non-compliance to Shariah. Though it was also stated that "the proceeds of the trust assets (as defined in

Condition 4 of the *'Terms and Conditions of the Sukuk Certificates—trust'*) are the sole source of payment on the *Sukuk* Certificates and the net proceeds of the realization of, or enforcement with respect to the trust assets may not be sufficient to make all payments due in respect of the *Sukuk* Certificates." (p. 1–2, the offering circular).

The third trick was *Post-Enforcement Payment Cascade:* In case of bankruptcy or early winding up, the Security Agent was to use the amounts recovered as a result of the enforcement of the Security Package to make payments in a sequential order. First, toward the amounts due and payable to (A) the agents, then (B) costs undertakings in the project (which is a normal order to pay the dues of outside parties first). Then it will make (C) payment of any Periodic Distribution Amounts due but unpaid under the *Sukuk* certificates; then (D) payment of any outstanding principal amounts under the *Sukuk* certificates; and then (E) a payment to RSRED.[9]

This sequencing of C, D, and E is only in line with an interest-bearing debt contract where the interest payment comes before the repayment of the principal. Had it been a *Musharakah*, then C, D, and E would have been treated together. The two parties (*Sukuk* holders and the RSRED) would have shared the residual in proportion to their capital contributions.

7.3 Use and Misuse of Trust Structure

An important feature of the Villamar *Sukuk* structure was creation of a trust to hold assets on behalf of the *sukuk* holders. The issuer acted in the capacity of a trustee and an agent of the *sukuk* holders to invest in the *Musharakah* as one partner, the other partner in the *Musharakah* being the RSRED. The trust not only held the *Musharakah* shares on behalf of the *sukuk* holders and passed the profits and losses to the *sukuk* holders, but it also served to keep an impenetrable separation between the *sukuk* holders and the project assets.

The offering circular states that: "Each *Sukuk* Certificate evidences an undivided beneficial ownership in the trust assets calculated pro rata based on the face value of the *Sukuk* Certificates (as defined in Condition 4.1 (Summary of the trust) and will rank pari passu, without any preference, with the other *Sukuk* Certificates".

"Once the Declaration of Trust has been declared, the *Sukuk* Certificates will represent a beneficial right to the trust assets held by the trustee on trust for the benefit of the Certificate holders. The recourse of the Certificate holders against the issuer or trustee is limited to the proceeds from the trust assets and once the trust assets have been realized and applied, the Certificate holders shall have no further rights against the issuer or trustee."[10]

The "trust" comprised of specific assets: issuer's shares in the *Musharakah*, income receivable from the *Musharakah*, and a security (mortgage) package contributed by the RSRED. The *sukuk* holders' recourse to the assets, in the event of loss or discontinuity of *Musharakah* business, if incurred without any fault or negligence of the *Musharakah* Manager, was made limited to the assets of this trust only. Not to the *Musharakah* or its project or its partners.

Creation of a trust or an SPV in Ijarah *sukuk* is understandable to create a bankruptcy remoteness between the obligor and the assets which are sold and leased, the subject matter of Ijarah *sukuk*. Should there be remoteness between the partners and the assets of the partnership even in case of bankruptcy? That is, should partners not have a recourse to the partnership assets in case of winding up of the partnership? What are the consequences of such non-recourse? These important questions have not received adequate attention in the literature on *Musharakah sukuk*.

To understand the consequences, let us see the transformation of the balance sheet of the trust and the balance sheet of the *sukuk* holders from initial issuance of the *sukuk* to an event of bankruptcy or abrupt closing of the business. Figure 2 shows this transformation at various stages. For simplicity of illustration, we have assumed away the additional securities, guarantees, and overcollateralization assets in the trust and focused on primary assets and liabilities of the *sukuk* deal.

In its current form, with the trust structure in place and a final recourse of *sukuk* holders only to the *Musharakah* shares, these *Musharakah sukuk* are analogous to the restricted certificates over

	trust		*Ṣukūk* holders	
	Assets	Liabilities	Assets	Liabilities
When money collected but not yet invested	+ *Ṣukūk* Proceeds	Debt to *Ṣukūk* holders	+ Credit to issuer (-) Price Paid for *Ṣukūk*	0
When investment in *Mushārakah* takes place	+ *Mushārakah* Shares (-) *Ṣukūk* Sale Proceeds	+ *Mushārakah* Shares (-) Debt to *Ṣukūk* holders	+ *Ṣukūk* (-) Credit to issuer	0
After the bankruptcy of underlying project	Residual net Assets of the underlying project	*Mushārakah* Shares	+ *Mushārakah* Shares (-) *Ṣukūk*	0

Fig. 2 Balance sheets of the trust and the *Ṣukūk* holders at different stages

Musharakah shares in which the holder of the derivative financial product never has recourse to the underlying real asset. Thus, Musharakah *sukuk* would be financial derivatives only and therefore subject to very different rules, not same as *sukuk*.

7.4 Trust and Its Governance Issues

There were several governance and operations issues in the trust created by the issuer in the Villamar *Sukuk*. The trust created was not fit and proper for the purpose. It suffered from many weaknesses of legal, incentives, and powers that rendered it incapable of safeguarding the interests of the *sukuk* holders; thus, it was no more than a paper tiger. For example, if we raise the questions such as:

What is the Declaration of Trust and what are its terms and conditions? What does it say about the rights and responsibilities of the trustees? Who will pay for the work of the trust? What legal protections does the trust have under the trust laws of the issuer entity country and the trust laws of the country where the *sukuk* assets are located? We find that:

a. The law in Bahrain where the Declaration of Trust was made, there exists a trust law since 2006 (Decree Law No.23/2006), applicable to

trusts registered with Central Bank of Bahrain (CBB). In such trusts, the CBB acts as supervisory authority. However, the trust declared for Villamar sukuk was not registered with the CBB and hence as such lacked proper enforcement power. The Declaration of Trust had only a moral standing with no legal enforceability. The offering circular state this as follows:
"The trust Law (Decree Law No. 23/2006) provides that only if:

(a) a trustee is licensed in that capacity by the Central Bank of Bahrain (the 'CBB'); and
(b) the trust itself is registered with the CBB,

then the CBB has supervisory powers over the trust. As the Declaration of Trust is, to that extent, informal, it is not certain that the terms thereof would be enforced by the Courts of Bahrain. However, the obligations of the issuer under the Declaration of Agency to act on behalf of the Certificate holders in accordance with their instructions (given in accordance with the terms and conditions of the Sukuk Certificates) are enforceable as a matter of contract under the laws of Bahrain"[11] (emphasis by underlining added).

b. A review of the terms and conditions and powers and responsibilities of the trustees shows that the trustees had no power to act independently. Even in case of a Termination Event or a Dissolution Event, the trustee cannot take independent action without the directives from the Transaction Administrator. Moreover, the sukuk holders were not able to ask the trustee for settlement proceedings, but they could only approach through the Transaction Administrator. There are both pros and cons of this approach. The pros are that the decision-making shifts from the local trustee (who may be influenced by the powerful originator/government) to the Transaction Administrator who may be an international bank not influenced by the local pressures. The cons are that the sukuk holders do not have a say in matters of bankruptcy settlement.
c. The opposite party in the deal structure paid the cost of operations of the trust and the trustees, i.e., RSRED who were the second partner as well as the project manager paid for the trust. With these conflict of interests, how could the trustees work for the safeguard of the *sukuk* holders' interests?

The trust's assets, which were in the beginning the proceeds from the sale of *sukuk*, were immediately (implicitly) exchanged for a stream of LIBOR + premium secured by a mortgage and a line of financing. The term implicit exchange is valid because of the way in which the shares of the issuer were defined, that these will have claim to an income stream linked to LIBOR in case of upside performance of the project, though paid from the revenues of the project. These shares of the issuer were part of the portfolio of the trust. The other asset in the trust was a claim to the Security Package in case of downside of the project, paid through invoking the securities/guarantees not necessarily through the liquidation of the project assets. A normal share would be defined as undivided interest in the assets of the project and an income stream defined by a percentage of the profit.

Ideally the trust is to safeguard the interests of both parties, but in the present case, it did not have enough powers and authority to negotiate on behalf of the *sukuk* holders or to liquidate the underlying assets in case of bankruptcy of the project.

8 Some Lessons

A summary evaluation of the *Musharakah*-based Villamar *Sukuk* is given in the Appendix where the *sukuk* structure is evaluated for various properties and conditions that commensurate with *Musharakah sukuk*. The summary shows that this *sukuk* had many desirable properties and conditions built into its structure; however, it failed to be a *Musharakah* on a number of key requirements and conditions.

The successful subscription of the Villamar *Sukuk* shows that the lending investors desired a lending instrument (competitive returns and principal secured) and the borrowing debtors desired a debt instrument. However, at the same time, both the lenders and borrower also wanted to "feel" that they are abiding by Shariah. This contradictory behavior (pursuit of worldly desires and lip service to religion) cannot bring the fruits of Islamic finance to the society. It shows a weakness in society that has to be addressed by all stakeholders at their respective level of work.

Interest-bearing debt has inherent conflict of interest between the lender and the borrower, which gives rise to stark differences in the behaviors of the two parties in the event of default or bankruptcy. The profit sharing (*Musharakah*) does not give rise to the same type of conflict of interest between the two partners. If same conflicts arise in *Musharakah*, then this is an indication of some flaw in the product structuring or its implementation despite its formulation as partnership.

Creating a trust and appointing the trustees without endowing them with necessary independence and powers to protect the interests of the beneficiaries will not be helpful. Rather such trust itself becomes a source of delay in resolution of bankruptcy. The party managing the project often has better opportunities to get information about impending problems or increasing prospects of the project ahead of the other non-managing partner. This information asymmetry can result in a strategic behavior by the informed party to the detriment of the many individual *sukuk* holders. Therefore, to increase the social impact of the *sukuk* and keep the adverse strategic behavior in control, there is a need to provide collective bargaining power to the *sukuk* holders. A trust, which is proactive, independent, and endowed with appropriate powers to protect the interest of *sukuk* holders, will be more beneficial than a trust only to create a separation of assets.

In a partnership *sukuk* (*Musharakah sukuk*), the remoteness between the partners and the assets of the project can be made for the normal course of business. However, this remoteness has to vanish in case of bankruptcy or early winding up of the partnership.

There are social, economic, and religious consequences of the kind of non-recourse tolerated in Villamar *Sukuk*. First, it contributed to delay in resolution and hence the economic losses in terms of potential other uses of the assets and property. It also kept the assets concentrated and frozen with one partner (RSRED) to the exclusion of a large number of *sukuk* holders who could not utilize it.

By not launching a true *Musharakah Sukuk* but structuring it as de facto debt certificate through roundabout methods, an important opportunity of attracting a different type of investors was lost. The opportunity to make market correction in the pricing of real estate was also lost. Advantages of Islamic finance are lost when Shariah-compliant finance is rendered ambiguous to the finance community and the public at large.

There is a need to create appropriate bankruptcy and resolution regime that will facilitate smooth and quick resolution of *sukuk*.

Notes

1. See for example, Al-Amine, Muhammad Al-Bashir (2008), and Ali, Salman Syed (2008).
2. Even in the year 2009, the company's income largely consisted of fair value gain (US$13.5 million) on investment property and no income from the sale of residential or commercial units. See http://www.reuters.com/article/2010/04/30/islamic-villamar-idUSLDE63T15S20100430.
3. The Gulf Holding statement came after its Residential South Real Estate unit's cash reserves fell to 5.45 million Bahraini dinars ($14.5 million) at the end of 2009 from 42.3 million a year earlier. http://www.reuters.com/article/2010/04/30/islamic-villamar-idUSLDE63T15S20100430.
4. "Bahrain-based Gulf Finance House (GFH) confirmed the signing of agreements with Gulf Holding Company and Al-Rajhi Bank for providing financing towards the completion of Villamar Project and restructuring of the existing *Sukuk* facility." News published on February, 20, 2015, at http://www.twentyfoursevennews.com/banking-finance/gfh-seeks-re-financing-for-villamar-project-ṣukūk/ (accessed on April 28, 2015).
5. "It reached an agreement with *sukuk* holders last week to push back repayment on US$110 million (Dh404m) of Islamic bonds for 6 years. The deal postpones a debt repayment that had been due next month. The bank is in the midst of overhauling its business model to generate steady sources of cash and ensure that its profits are less dependent on fee income from deals, said Hisham Alrayes, the bank's acting chief executive." [Source: http://www.thenational.ae/business/industry-insights/finance/islamic-bank-gulf-finance-house-seeks-better-times, accessed on April 24, 2015].
6. There was no objective valuation of the license to construct on the land. However, the land valuation was independently estimated. **Land Valuation:** The total cost for the land was BD33,222,636

(equivalent of US$88,123,042), consisting of the purchase price and related fees/commissions. The total current market value of the Land is estimated at: BD52,172,000 (equivalent of US$138,386,230); and BD32,143,000 (equivalent of US$85,259,307)—on a residual basis, according to a valuation report dated February 11, 2008, issued by DTZ Bahrain.

7. AAOIFI Standard 12 on Musharakah stipulates an agreed profit sharing ratio (clause 3/1/5/3) but allows for putting a ceiling on profit of one or more partners that any profit above that amount belongs to a particular partner (clause 3/1/5/9).
8. Though the guarantee to the issuer (partner) was partial as the size of the security package was smaller than the size of investment of the issuer (partner) in *Musharakah*.
9. Preliminary Offering Circular, p. 25.
10. Preliminary Offering Circular, p. 25.
11. Villamar Sukuk Offering Circular, p. 44. Full circular available at http://ae.zawya.com/researchreports/p_2006_10_19_10_26_01/20080520_p_2006_10_19_10_26_01_064922.pdf.

Villamar *Ṣukūk* Evaluation Matrix

(Matrix developed by author based on criteria of AAOIFI, IDEAL Ratings, and General Sharia Rules for *Mushārakah*)

Sharīʿah-process-effects	The feature is present in Sukuk offering document	Shariah compliance status		Comments
		Compliance on required aspects	Compliance on desirable aspects	
Ṣukūk structure utilizes common Islamic investment modes	Yes		✓	Partnership (*Mushārakah*)
Explicit obligation to Sharīah	Yes	✓		
Adequate disclosure of contractual conditions	Yes	✓		
Disclosure of loss conditions	Yes	✓		
Sharīʿah Board or auditor monitors implementation	No	✗		
Compliant use of proceeds by originator	Yes	✓		
Adequate disclosure of default conditions	Yes	✓		
Purchase undertaking agreement	No	✓		N/A as the asset is on-sold to third party

(continued)

Sharīʿah-process-effects	The feature is present in Sukuk offering document	Shariah compliance status		Comments
		Compliance on required aspects	Compliance on desirable aspects	
Sale undertaking agreement	No	✓		N/A as the asset is on-sold to third party
The *Ṣukūk* is approved by a Sharīʿah Board	Yes	✓		
Limited recourse to issuer	Yes	✓		Issuer was the trustee
Exercise price is a market price or NAV	Not applicable			
Profit distributions from the trust assets	Yes	✓		
Manager is obliged to make up profit shortfalls	No	✓		
Manager seizes surplus profits	Yes		✗	
Manager borrows from reserve account for his own interest	Not applicable			
Ṣukūk holders have full rights of asset disposition	No	✗		

(continued)

Sharīʿah-process-effects	The feature is present in Sukuk offering document	Shariah compliance status		Comments
		Compliance on required aspects	Compliance on desirable aspects	
In case of dissolution the *Ṣukūk* holders receive residual value of the project in proportion of their share in the project	Ambiguous No/Yes	✗ / ✓		Page 26. **Redemption following a Dissolution Event:** The *Ṣukūk* Certificates may be redeemed in full prior to the Scheduled Dissolution Date upon the occurrence of a Dissolution Event, as further described in Condition 10 (*Dissolution of trust*) Each *Ṣukūk* Certificate will be redeemed at the aggregate principal amount of such *Ṣukūk* Certificate then outstanding plus any accrued and unpaid Periodic Distribution Amounts as at such date **Whereas Page 57 states that:** 3.2.2 The net proceeds of the realisation of, or enforcement with respect to, the trust Assets may not be sufficient to make all payments due in respect of the Sukuk Certificates. **If, following distribution of such proceeds, there remains a shortfall in payments due under the Sukuk Certificates,** subject to Condition 14 (Enforcement and Exercise of Rights), no Certificateholder will have any claim against the issuer, the trustee, the Arranger, the Co-Lead Managers, the Placement Agents, the Transaction Administrator, the Agents, the Security Agent, the Account Bank, the Investment Manager or the Developers (to the extent that they have fulfilled all of their obligations under the relevant Transaction Documents to which they are a party) or any of their affiliates or other assets in respect of such shortfall and **any unsatisfied claims of Certificateholders shall be extinguished**

(continued)

Sharīʿah-process-effects	The feature is present in Sukuk offering document	Shariah compliance status		Comments
		Compliance on required aspects	Compliance on desirable aspects	
Clear specification of the underlying asset	Yes	✓		
Profit share is predefined ratio of actual profits	No	✗		Pre defined LIBOR + margin for the issuer Profit sharing ratio of Musharik-2 (RSRED) is not predefined, it continuously increases with profit
English law as governing law	Yes		✗	
Musharik-1 is liable for capital loss and/or less profits	Yes and No	✓		Muhsarik-1 is issuer. It is lesser exposed to losses (due to Security Package) than Musharik-2
Musharik-2 is liable for capital loss and/or less profits	Yes	✓		Musharik-2 is RSRED. More exposed to losses if they occur
All *Mushārakah* partners are liable to losses in proportion to their capital	No	✗		Musharik-1 is less exposed to loss than Musharik-2 due to existence of security Package for Musharik-1
Scope of *Mushārakah* is clear	Yes	✓		To construct buildings on a well-defined piece of land and on-sell these to third parties

(continued)

Sharīʿah-process-effects	The feature is present in Sukuk offering document	Shariah compliance status		Comments
		Compliance or required aspects	Compliance on desirable aspects	
No debt in *Mushārakah* capital	Yes	✓		Though one party is contributing only a license permission and a letter of credit
In-Kind capital contribution to *Mushārakah* valued at market rate	No	✗		Privately agreed value of construction license. No assessment whether the valuation is fair or not
Bankruptcy procedures well defined in the offering document	Yes	✓		
Bankruptcy procedures according to Sharīʿah	No	✗		Page 26. **Redemption following a Dissolution Event:** The *Şukūk* Certificates may be redeemed in full prior to the Scheduled Dissolution date upon the occurrence of a Dissolution Event, as further described in Condition 10 (*Dissolution of Trust*) Each *Şukūk* Certificate will be redeemed at the aggregate principal amount of such *Şukūk* Certificate then outstanding plus any accrued and unpaid Periodic Distribution Amounts as at such date

References

Al-Amine, M. A.-B. (2008). Sukuk market: Innovations and challenges. In S. S. Ali (Ed.), *Islamic capital markets: Products, regulation and development.* Jeddah: Islamic Research and Training Institute.

Ali, S. S. (2008). Islamic capital markets: Current state and development challenges. In *Islamic capital markets: Products, regulation and development.* Jeddah: Islamic Research and Training Institute.

Salah, O. (2010). Dubai debt crisis: A legal analysis of the Nakheel Sukuk. *Berkeley Journal of International Law, 4,* 19–32. Available at http://papers.ssrn.com/sol3/papers.cfm?abstract_id=1663276.

Van Wijnbergen, S., & Zaheer S. (2013). Sukuk defaults: On distress resolution in Islamic finance. Available at http://papers.ssrn.com/sol3/papers.cfm?abstract_id=2293938.

Villamar Sukuk. Prospectus and preliminary offering circular. Available at http://ae.zawya.com/researchreports/p_2006_10_19_10_26_01/20080520_p_2006_10_19_10_26_01_064922.pdf.

News Websites

Reuters. Gulf Holding says no cash crunch at Villamar sukuk. Published April 30, 2010 at http://www.reuters.com/article/2010/04/30/islamic-villamar-idUSLDE63T15S20100430. Accessed on 22 April 2015.

Twenty-four/Seven News. GFH seeks re-financing for Villamar project, Sukuk. News published on 20 February 2015 at http://www.twentyfoursevennews.com/banking-finance/gfh-seeks-re-financing-for-villamar-project-ṣukūk/ Accessed on 28 April 2015.

The National. Islamic bank Gulf Finance House seeks better times. News published on 26 May 2015 at http://www.thenational.ae/business/industry-insights/finance/islamic-bank-gulf-finance-house-seeks-better-times. Accessed 24 April 2015.

Towards a Robust *Shariah* Screening Criterion for Stocks

Farrukh Habib

Abstract If it was not for the indices for *Shariah* compliant equities, the global Islamic capital market (ICM) would not have proliferated with an astounding pace. Those indices have played an extremely crucial role in assisting the investors seeking *Shariah* compliant stocks to invest their capital. This conjecture is equally true for Pakistan. In this regard, a remarkable initiative recently taken by the country is the launch of All Shares Islamic Index of Pakistan (ASIIP). The index has been established to develop Pakistan's ICM and to cater the needs of the investors pursuing *Shariah* compliant investment in stocks. The selection criterion of ASIIP comprises of mainly two categories: (1) *Shariah* screening criterion and (2) technical filters. Although a general understanding has been established regarding the *Shariah* screening criterion and its conceptual basis, there seems to always linger a muddle about how those *Shariah* rulings are unswervingly related to it. Part of this confusion is attributable to the presence of rather an incongruity between the criterion and its *Shariah* underpinnings. In view of that, this paper gives

F. Habib (✉)
International Shariah Research Academy, Kuala Lumpur, Malaysia
e-mail: farrukh@isra.my

S.A.R. Rizvi and I. Saba (eds.), *Developments in Islamic Finance*, Palgrave CIBFR Studies in Islamic Finance, DOI 10.1007/978-3-319-59342-5_5

an insightful discussion on the criterion from *Shariah* perspective. It critically analyses the criterion and its underlying *Shariah* basis by conducting a comprehensive and conscientious research through qualitative method. In doing so, it also juxtaposes the criterion directly to the classical sources of Islamic jurisprudence. On the basis of analysis, it proposes major modifications, on the one hand, to introduce a new ratio or filter within the criterion and, on the other hand, to exclude unnecessary ones from it. It also recommends re-examining the benchmarks for the prevalent ratios. These propositions would not only improve the robustness of the prevailing criterion, but also help abridging the gap between practical aspect of the criterion and its conceptual *Shariah* basis. Ultimately, it would vitally contribute to critical success factors and future progression of ICM in Pakistan.

Keywords All Shares Islamic Index of Pakistan (ASIIP) · Islamic capital market (ICM) · Islamic law · *Fiqh*

1 Introduction

Islamic capital market (ICM) is an integral part of Islamic financial system without which Islamic finance would have faced great difficulty in delivering its value proposition of profit and loss sharing, circulation of wealth, promoting business partnerships, and stimulating real economic activities. In fact, the concept of "risk sharing" which has gained popularity lately as the essence of Islamic finance inculcates asset-backed equity financing and participation in mobilising economic resources in order to utilise them in the most efficient way for the sake of realising social justice and economic development. One of the most significant means for boosting the idea of risk-sharing is through strengthening the ICM which would subsequently facilitate participation of a vast group of investors towards economic growth and prosperity (Maghrebi and Mirakhor 2015).

Due to the crucial importance of ICMs, many countries, like Malaysia, Indonesia, Bahrain, UAE and Saudi Arabia, have already established their own markets, while they are keenly putting their efforts to further develop them into more resilient, deeper and global ones. On the contrary, Pakistan is yet to develop its ICM as equities and *sukuk* issuances are still comparatively few in the country. Nevertheless, the country has shown sincere interest, braced by huge domestic demand, to grow in the area (IFSB 2016).

One of the critical success factors of the ICM in Pakistan is the launch of KSE-Meezan Index 30 (KMI-30) in September 2008. More recently, All Shares Islamic Index of Pakistan (ASIIP) has also been introduced in November 2015, which is a milestone in the development of ICM at the domestic level. Both the indices measure performance of equities listed at the Pakistan Stock Exchange (PSX), except with a difference that KMI-30 only tracks thirty most liquid *Shariah* compliant companies listed on PSX, while ASIIP tracks all *Shariah* compliant companies that are listed at the same stock exchange. Nevertheless, the *Shariah* screening criterion for both the indices is exactly the same (PSX 2015a, b).

The criterion of both indices comprises mainly of two categories of filters: (1) *Shariah* screening criterion and (2) technical filters. It is the former category which is the focus of this paper. Although a general understanding has been established regarding the screening criterion and its *Shariah* basis, due to lack of any quality research, it remains ambiguous that how such screening criterion is directly related to its *Fiqhi* basis and *Shariah* rulings. Moreover, there is a need to critically analyse the criterion itself against its *Shariah* underpinnings in order to eliminate any potential incongruity. In view of that, this paper gives an insightful discussion on the criterion from *Shariah* perspective. Furthermore, it critically analyses the criterion and its underlying *Shariah* basis by conducting a comprehensive and conscientious research through the utilisation of the method of qualitative documentary analysis.

In order to achieve this objective, this paper is organised in the following manner. It starts with an introduction, followed by a description of the *Shariah* screening criterion of ASIIP. It then delves into a methodical discussion and critical analysis of *Fiqhi* and logical basis of the filters in the screening criterion of ASIIP one by one. After that, it presents a proposal for introducing a new and unique filter in the criterion in order to make it more rigorous and comprehensive. Finally, the paper ends with a conclusion and momentous recommendations.

2 *Shariah* Screening Criterion of ASIIP and KMI-30

The *Shariah* screening criterion of ASIIP and KMI-30 consists of mainly six filters. They are as follows:

1. Business of the Investee Company
2. Non-Compliant Income to Total Revenue, <5%
3. Non-Compliant Investments to Total Assets, <33%
4. Interest-Bearing Debt to Total Assets, <37%
5. Illiquid Assets to Total Assets, >25%
6. Net Liquid Assets/Share Vs Market Price/Share

These filters are categorised in Table 1 below:

As shown in Table 1 above, this paper divides the *Shariah* screening criterion of ASIIP into two categories: (1) filters for screening impermissible (haram) activities and assets, which can be called compliance filters, and (2) filters for tradability (negotiability) of shares, which can be called tradability filters. The reason for such categorisation will become clearer in the later discussion. However, it is adequate to mention here that the first type of filters are employed to ensure that a company's business activities and assets are permissible from *Shariah* perspective, or at least impermissible activities and assets remain within a tolerable benchmark. The second type of filters warrants that the trading of shares that pass first type of filters is allowed without attracting the *Shariah* rulings of currency exchange and sale of debt (receivables). All these filters will be discussed sequentially in the next section.

Table 1 *Shariah* screening criterion Of ASIIP and KMI-30

Categories of filters	Name of filters	Purpose of filters	Benchmark of filters
Compliance filters	Business of the investee company	To exclude companies with impermissible or unethical core business	Businesses based on interest or *riba* (i.e., conventional banks), *gharar* (i.e., insurance companies), gambling (i.e., casinos), manufacturers or traders of impermissible products (i.e., liquor, pork, and haram meat), while tobacco and arms and weaponry businesses are excluded on ethical grounds;
	Non-compliant income to total revenue	To control interest and other types of impermissible income	Impermissible + interest income <5% of total revenue
	Non-compliant investments to total assets	To control involvement in non-compliant investments and interest-taking deposits	Non-compliant investments and interest taking deposits <33% of the total asset
	Interest bearing debt to total assets	To control interest-bearing debt	Interest-bearing debt <37% of the total asset
Tradability filters	Illiquid assets to total assets	To ensure that illiquid assets are in substantial amount	Illiquid assets >25% of the total asset
	Net liquid assets/share vs market price/share	To ensure that liquid assets are sold at par	Market price = or > net liquid assets

Source Constructed from PSX (2015a, b)

3 *Fiqhi* and Logical Basis of the Screening Criterion

Under compliance category, there are a total of four filters, whereas under tradability category, there are only two filters. Their *Fiqhi* and logical basis are discussed in this section. In doing so, this section also provides a critical analysis of those filters and accordingly recommends for further improvements.

3.1 Business of the Investee Company

According to PSX (2015a), it is a requirement for a company to be *Shariah* compliant that its core business should not violate any principle of *Shariah* regarding permissible and impermissible activities. Consequently, conventional banks, insurance companies, companies that are involved in manufacturing or trading of impermissible products, like pork and alcohol, or providing impermissible services, like pornography, etc., will be disqualified from the list of *Shariah* compliant companies. This basic requirement is quite clear, because investing in companies whose main business activity is impermissible is not allowed. Investing in such companies would mean that the investors (shareholders) not only own, but also promote their activity. That is impermissible based on the verse of Quran:

> Help one another to do what is right and good; do not help one another towards sin and hostility. (Quran, Al-Ma`idah, 5:2, Translation by Abdul Haleem 2004)

Likewise, the revenue generated from any impermissible activity is also impermissible based on the collective understanding of the Islamic legal maxims, which are stated as follows:

> Whatever is based on invalid is invalid [itself]. (Al-Zuhayli 2006, vol. 1, p. 457)
>
> Whatever is impermissible, its price is also impermissible. (Al-Zuhayli 2006, vol.1, p. 632)

> The revenue [generated from the original property] follows the [Shariah ruling of the] original property. (Al-Zuhayli 2006, vol. 1, p. 668)

> The dependent is not singled out for Shariah ruling. (Al-Zuhayli 2006, vol. 1, p. 441)

Al-Zuhayli (2006) explains that the above maxims are also applied in contracts and transactions. When a contract or transaction is considered as illegal from *Shariah* perspective, its constituents and outcome also become invalid because they are dependent on the contract or transaction itself. Therefore, companies with impermissible core business activities are excluded from the universe of *Shariah* compliant companies, as acquiring and trading of shares of such companies is also impermissible.

The requirement of core business activity filters out only those companies whose main businesses are impermissible; however, there are many companies whose primary businesses are permissible, but they are, one way or another, involved in some impermissible activities that are ancillary in nature: for instance, a company manufactures permissible product, but borrows capital from a conventional bank on interest or *riba*; it has interest-taking deposits in a conventional bank; or it has interest-bearing securities that generate interest income. Other examples include a hotel or airline which basically provides accommodation or transportation services, respectively, but also sells alcohol to their customers. A supermarket is another example which mainly sells permissible household products, but also vends pork, liquor and other impermissible items. It is difficult to filter out such mixed activities companies through the filter of core business. Therefore, the remaining three filters under the compliance category cater for such companies having mixed activities.

The basic *Shariah* ruling for mixed activities companies is that they are also non-*Shariah* compliant. Acquiring and trading of shares of such companies is not permissible as well. This is the opinion held by the Islamic *Fiqh* Academy of OIC[1] in its resolution no. 63/1/7, dated May 1992, and Islamic *Fiqh* Council of Muslim World League in its 4th resolution of 14th session, dated January 1995. However, it is a fact that in the contemporary world, it is very difficult to find a company whose activities are all completely *Shariah* compliant (Khatkhatay and

Nisar 2007; Usmani 2011). Strictly following this opinion would enact hardship on general public and hamper the growth of Islamic finance. AAOIFI (2015) elaborates that it is a situation of "`*umum balwa*"[2] which would impose general hardship on the public. Hence, exempting mixed activities companies from this opinion of prohibition would promote removal of hardship. However, this exemption is only given to those companies that would adhere to certain conditions or parameters.

Recognising this issue, AAOIFI (2015), SAC-SCM (2006), *Shariah* boards of various institutions and individual scholars, like Sheikh Taqi Usmani (2007, 2011, 2015a), Sheikh Yusuf Al-Shubily (2015), Sheikh Hussein Hamid Hassan (2015), Sheikh Ali El-Gari (1998, 2015), Sheikh Muhammad Bin Othaymeen and Sheikh Abdullah Bin Al-Mavi (cited by Mansoori and Khan 2015), and many others allow to exempt companies from this basic *Shariah* ruling which fulfil certain conditions.

The remaining three filters under the compliance category of ASIIP are essentially the conditions that exempt mixed activities companies from the basic *Shariah* ruling of prohibition of such companies and their shares. However, it is important to note that exempting those mixed activities companies from the ruling of prohibition is a concession. Such concession does not render their impermissible activities as permissible. Therefore, the objective of those conditions is to minimise and control the involvement of companies in impermissible activities to the minimum possible level.

3.2 Non-Compliant Income to Total Revenue

According to PSX (2015a), it is a requirement for companies that their *Shariah* non-compliant income should not exceed 5% of the total revenue. The non-compliant income can be in the form of interest income, income from production or sale of prohibited products or services, any late payment charges from a credit sale, dividend income from prohibited companies, etc.

Usmani (2015b) discussed a similar benchmark of income from non-*Shariah* compliant activities in the context of investment in equity funds. He remarked that the percentage limit of this filter has been derived purely through *ijtihad* of the contemporary scholars as there is no basis in the main sources of *Shariah* for this specific percentage limit.

The same limit of 5% of total revenue or income for impermissible income has also been adopted by other various institutions, like AAOIFI (2015), SAC-SCM (2013),[3] S&P (2015), FTSE (2015) and MSCI (2015). It can be argued that prohibition of interest and income from other impermissible sources is explicitly mentioned in *Shariah*; hence, it cannot be allowed even at less than 5% level. It is indeed a valid objection. However, it can be responded with the argument that such concession is only given based on the concept of removal of hardship and dire need. This is supported by an Islamic legal maxim as follows:

> Hardship begets ease. (Al-Zuhayli 2006, vol. 1, p. 257)

It means that imposition of hardship on general public should be avoided. When hardship is observed, provisions should be made to facilitate matters and make ease for the general public. Another maxim states as follows:

> Necessity permits forbidden things. (Al-Zuhayli 2006, vol. 1, p. 276)

This maxim indicates that the ruling of proscriptions in *Shariah* can be temporarily changed due to dire need. On the basis of those maxims, it is assumed that if impermissible income is less than 5% of the total revenue, it can be negligible with a condition that later it would be cleansed from the dividend paid and channelled to charity by the investors (Usmani 2011). Moreover, it can be further added that things which are rare, small or paltry can be neglected in taking into consideration for *Shariah* ruling based on the following maxim:

> Consideration [in issuing Shariah ruling] is given to the predominant and widespread, not to the paltry and rare. (Al-Zuhayli 2006, vol. 1, p. 325)

Since the share of impermissible income in total revenue can only be 5% at maximum, it can be considered as insignificant against 95% of the predominant permissible income. However, it needs to be re-emphasised here that the impermissible income does not become permissible due to its trivial amount. It is only tolerable due to its small amount and pervasive nature; that is why the shareholders are required to cleanse such impermissible income from dividend payments (Usmani 2011).

Although such line of argument seems to be valid, there is a problem with setting the limit of impermissible income at 5% of the total revenue. It should be well conceived at this juncture that the issue of interest or *riba* is taken very seriously in *Shariah*, as the Holy Quran says as follows:

> But those who take usury will rise up on the Day of Resurrection like someone tormented by Satan's touch. That is because they say, 'Trade and usury are the same,' but God has allowed trade and forbidden usury. Whoever, on receiving God's warning, stops taking usury may keep his past gains– God will be his judge– but whoever goes back to usury will be an inhabitant of the Fire, there to remain. God blights usury, but blesses charitable deeds with multiple increase: He does not love the ungrateful sinner. (Quran, Al-Baqarah, 2:275–276, Translation by Abdul Haleem 2004)

Based on the above verses of Quran, in an ideal situation, the original percentage limit for this filter should be 0%. One cannot be careful enough when making concession for *riba* from the strict prohibition mentioned above. Moreover, custom (*al-`urf*) and practice (*al-`adah*) of the people are well-established basis for *ijtihad*. They are recognised and acknowledged by *Shariah* as long as they meet certain conditions and do not contradict with any explicit ruling. One of the fundamental Islamic legal maxims validates the importance of custom in deriving *Shariah* rulings as follows:

> Customary practice is a determining factor [in issuing a Shariah ruling]. (Al-Zuhayli 2006, vol. 1, p. 298)

Therefore, it is vital to carefully check whether or not the limit of 5% of the total revenue for interest and impermissible income is appropriate, is supported by custom and practice of the people and rested on sufficient evidence of necessity. On the one hand, the restriction cannot be too stringent that it could not serve the purpose of making concession; on the other hand, it cannot be too relaxed that it would allow people to involve in prohibited things beyond their requisites, because according to an Islamic legal maxim:

> Necessity must be limited only to its proportion. (Al-Zuhayli 2006, vol. 1, p. 281)

The above maxim is basically a restriction of the previously mentioned maxim which says that at the time of necessity, forbidden things can be allowed. So, by combining both the maxims, it is construed that prohibited things can be allowed when a valid necessity arises to do so, but such allowance should be restricted to the proportion of the necessity itself. Indeed, such allowance cannot be used beyond that necessity.

A study by Khatkhatay and Nisar (2007) reveals that when the limit of 5% of the total revenue for interest and impermissible income was applied on shares of the companies in BSE 500,[4] almost 90% of the companies qualified for the *Shariah* compliant list. When the limit of just 1% was applied, still almost 75% of the companies passed the criterion. Their empirical evidence validated that the limit of 5% was too relaxed for the companies in BSE 500. Based on their findings, they suggested to have the limit of not more than 3% of the total revenue for interest and impermissible income. Drawing from the conclusion of their study, it is proposed that a comprehensive empirical research should also be conducted on the companies listed in PSX to check the aptness of 5% limit. It is very much desirable if the 5% limit could be further reduced to a lower percentage supported by the findings of the research, because in this way, the condition of limiting the necessity to its proportionate level could be fulfilled. In fact, a policy should be designed to assess suitability of the prevalent percentage limit of the filter on a regular basis, so that it could be gradually decreased to the ideal percentage, which is 0%.

3.3 Non-compliant Investments to Total Assets

According to PSX (2015a), it is a requirement for ASIIP that the non-compliant investments of a company should be less than 33% of its total assets. Such investment consists of conventional mutual funds, money market instruments, commercial papers, interest-bearing deposits, bonds, derivatives and others. Moreover, it also comprises of investment in companies that are not in the list of *Shariah* compliant companies.

This filter seems to provide another layer of restriction for involvement in impermissible activities. It basically complements the filter of non-compliant income to total revenue. So the filter of non-compliant income to total revenue discourages companies from involving in impermissible activities by keeping a check on the income generated through those activities. While the filter of non-compliant investments to total assets tries to achieve the same objective by limiting their amount of investments, this filter also seems to have been constructed through *ijtihad* based on the rules of *`umum balwa*, removal of hardship, and principal of primacy and dependency. While the rules of *`umum balwa* and removal of hardship are quite evident in such situation, it is appropriate to elaborate the principal of primacy and dependency here. The principle is stated as follows:

> The subordinate [of a principal factor] is [considered as] subordinate [in Shariah ruling as well]. (Al-Zuhayli 2006, vol. 2, p. 689)

The above maxim stipulates that whatever is subordinate to a principal thing or factor should take up the *Shariah* ruling of the principal, unless it contradicts another established *Shariah* ruling regarding the subordinate. One of the extensions of the above maxim is stated as follows:

> Those things which cannot be marginalized [in issuing Shariah rulings] when they are independent, can be overlooked when they are subsidiary [to another independent factor]. (Al-Zuhayli, vol. 2, p. 689)

Since non-compliant investment of a company is not intended in acquiring and trading of its shares, especially when they are limited to only 33% of the total assets, they can be considered as subsidiary. Due to their subservient nature, they can be overlooked in forming the *Shariah* ruling of acquiring and trading of shares of that company.

This filter is also common in other criteria and indexes. For instance, SAC-SCM (2013) has a limit of 33% of the total assets of the company on interest-taking deposits. Similarly, AAOIFI (2015) has 30% of the market capitalisation of the company. In addition, DJIMI (2015), S&P (2015), FTSE (2015) and MSCI (2015) also have filters analogous to this filter with some slight differences.

As for the number (33%) of limit, it seems that it has been derived from a hadith, which is stated as follows:

> Saad Bin Abi Waqas (R.A.) narrates: "I said: O Allah's Apostle (صلى الله عليه وسلم)! May I bequeath all my property (in charity)? He said: No. I said: Then may I bequeath half of it? He said: No. I said: One third? He said: Yes, one third, yet even one third is too much. It is better for you to leave your inheritors wealthy than to leave them poor begging others, and whatever you spend for Allah's sake will be considered as a charitable deed even the handful of food you put in your wife's mouth." (Al-Bukhari 2001, hadith # 2742)

Some scholars understand from the above hadith that one-third amount of anything can be considered as major or abundant. The aptness of deriving the rule of one-third (33%) as being majority or abundant based on the above hadith is very controversial among the scholars. Hanafi scholars do not give credence to this rule. According to them, the criterion of majority is more than half (>50%), and minority is less than half (<50%). And the criterion of something that is exactly half (=50%) should be decided on the basis of custom (*al-`urf*) (Al-Kasani 1986). Al-Nadwi (2006) commented that Hanafi's criterion is more rational than the rule of one-third. Therefore, instead of relying on the rule of one-third or the criterion of majority, the number of limits should be based on the concept of necessity. Accordingly, it needs to be justified on the basis of empirical evidence. A research should be conducted on the companies listed in PSX for determining the exact percentage limit for this filter on the basis of necessity and removal of hardship.

3.4 Interest-Bearing Debt to Total Assets

According to PSX (2015a), it is a requirement for a company to be *Shariah* compliant that its interest-bearing debt should be less than 37% of its total assets. The interest-bearing debt includes bonds, commercial papers, loans from conventional banks, financial lease, hire purchase and preference shares.

Besides the fact that the filter is quite understandable, interestingly the brochure poorly explains the rationale behind this filter as follows:

> To understand the rationale behind this condition, it should be kept in mind that such companies are mostly based on interest. Here again, the aforementioned principle applies i.e. if the shareholder is not personally agreeable to such borrowings, but has been overruled by the majority, these borrowing transactions cannot be attributed to him/her. (PSX, 2015a, p. 3)

It is not clear what does "such companies" mean in the above statement. Moreover, the part of the statement "such companies are mostly based on interest" is quite vague and confusing as well. The statement further talks about a previously mentioned principle, but the principle is not mentioned earlier in the brochure. However, a similar statement has been stated by Usmani (2015b) in the context of investment in equity funds, he mentions:

> If the main business of companies [with some non-Shariah compliant activities] is halal, like automobiles, textile, etc. but they deposit their surplus amounts in an interest-bearing account or borrow money on interest, the shareholder must express his disapproval against such dealings, preferably by raising his voice against such activities in the annual general meeting of the company. (Usmani 2015b, p. 288)

In another place, he comments as follows:

> [For the rationale behind debt to total asset ratio is that] such [mixed activities] companies sometimes borrow money from conventional

> financial institutions that are mostly based on interest. Here again, the aforementioned principle applies i.e. if a shareholder is not personally agreeable to such borrowings, but [his voice in the annual general meeting] has been overruled by the majority, these borrowing transactions cannot be attributed to him. (Usmani 2015b, p. 291)

It can be made out from the above statements that generally the companies are not allowed to borrow loans on interest from a *Shariah* point of view. However, if they do and shareholders do not personally approve such borrowing then such borrowing cannot be attributed to them.

This justification seems to be flawed. AAOIFI (2015) gives definition of a share as follows:

> A share represents an undivided share in the capital of a corporation, just as it represents an undivided share in its assets and the rights associated with it upon conversion of the capital into tangible things, benefits, debts, and so on. (AAOIFI 2015, *Shariah* Standard No. 21, para 3/1)

It can be construed from the above definition that the "rights associated with" the capital and assets of a corporation also belong to the shareholders. It is quite clear that the shareholders are the owners of the company. In fact, AAOIFI (2015) in *Shariah* Standard No. 12, para 4/1/1/1 and 4/1/1/2, explicitly describes shareholders of a company as its co-owners. Being the owners of the company and its activities, the company's activities are definitely attributable to them. It is very difficult to separate their personal opinion and their collective opinions and actions as the shareholders and owners of the company. Knowing that a company is going to take interest-bearing debt whenever it needs, pay interest on it and continue to do so, while at the same time, the investors are basically not only agreeing but also approving such practice of the company by subscribing to its shares in the primary market; How they cannot be held responsible?

The issue is similar when the investors buy shares in the secondary market, they also know that the company, whose shares they are buying, has already borrowed some loans on interest, and has been paying interest on it, so definitely it is attributable to them as well. Even if the investors personally disapprove such practice of the company, it does not matter at all. Usmani (2011, 2015b) mention that they may raise their voices against such practice of the company in annual general meetings or at any other platform, but they know that their demand would be rejected for sure by the majority of the shareholders. Yet, they buy shares of that company, receive dividends or obtain capital gains through trading its shares. In this situation, it is difficult not to think that such practice of the company is not attributable to its shareholders.

However, a more appropriate justification for tolerating the company's practice of borrowing loans on interest and paying interest on them rests on the concept of necessity and removal of hardship. Since the investors do not tend to focus on the interest-bearing debt at the time of acquiring and trading shares, it should be treated as subsidiary to the main subject matter of the transaction. Many scholars, like Aal Sheikh (1979), Al-Manea (1996), Al-Qurahdaghi (2003), Aal Sulayman (2006), Al-Yahya (2007) and others have pointed out that the main subject matter of the transaction in acquiring and trading shares is the company, its main business activities and operations, its assets, and its ability to generate revenue in future. As long as those factors are *Shariah* compliant, ancillary activities can be overlooked with the condition that they remain insignificant.

In the criterion of ASIIP, based on the filter of the business of the investee company, it can be ensured that the main business of the company does not involve interest-based transactions or impermissible activities. So the main business activities of the companies in ASIIP, which remained after applying that filter, focus only on the *Shariah* compliant manufacturing or providing permissible services. Borrowing loans on interest cannot be considered as their main business activity. In addition, the interest-bearing debt is also kept within the limit of 37% of the total assets of the company. Therefore, it can be tolerated.

The argument of tolerating a company's practice of borrowing loans on interest and paying interest on them based on the concept of necessity and removal of hardship seems to be valid. However, it is not clear how the percentage limit of 37% of the total assets of a company has been set for the filter. It cannot be said that it follows the rule of one-third because even according to that rule, it should be less than 33%.

When Usmani (2015b) suggested the rule of one-third for debt-to-total asset ratio for investment in equity funds, he also preferred to set the limit at 30% of the total assets, which is not more than one-third. In addition, 37% is also higher than many other criteria set by the global institutions. For instance, AAOIFI (2015) has set a limit of 30% of market capitalisation of a company for interest-bearing debt. SAC-SCM (2013) has 33% of the total assets as the limit for interest-bearing debt. In fact, DJIMI (2015), S&P (2015), take the whole debt of a company and restrict it at 33% of market capitalisation of the company, while FTSE (2015) and MSCI (2015) confine it at 33.33% of the total assets. Compared to those benchmarks, 37% seems to be a very liberal number. Therefore, an empirical research validating the necessity of such concession is strongly required.

3.5 Illiquid Assets to Total Assets

According to PSX (2015a), the illiquid assets of a company in the ASIIP should not be less than 25% of its total assets. The illiquid assets are defined in the brochure of PSX (2015a) as the assets which can be traded at any price. For instance, inventory of raw materials, work in process, property, plant, equipment and other fixed assets are considered illiquid. From this explanation, liquid assets can be defined as the assets which cannot be traded at any price, other than their par value, according to the principles of *Shariah*. The liquid assets of the company cannot exceed 75% of the total assets. They can mainly consist of cash, current accounts or cash equivalents held by a company. Moreover, receivables or any other financial rights also fall under this category.

Another point worth noting here is that the liquid assets in this filter do not confine to non-*Shariah* compliant assets only. It also includes *Shariah* compliant assets. For instance, a company has put cash of 32% of the total assets in a conventional bank, on which it earns interest of 4% of the total revenue. It has also put cash of 10% of the total assets into an Islamic bank. And it also has receivables of 34% of the total assets which have been established through *Shariah* compliant transactions (like *Murabaha* and *salam*). The company would pass the filter of non-compliant income to total revenue and the filter of non-compliant investments to total assets, but it would not pass the filter of illiquid assets to total assets, because its liquid assets, compliant and non-compliant combined, would become 76% of the total assets. In this way, the benchmark of illiquid assets to total assets, which is 25%, would not be met.

AAOIFI (2015) has set a similar filter in *Shariah* Standard No. 21, para 3/19, which limits liquid assets to 70% of the total assets. It means illiquid assets are required to be at least 30% of the total assets. Unlike PSX (2015a), AAOIFI (2015) provides a better elucidation of this filter. It says when all the assets of a company are in the form of cash, the trading of its shares can only be done at their nominal value and with the condition of delivery on spot. In other words, it has to follow the *Shariah* rules of currency exchange (*bay` al-sarf*). Likewise, if all the assets of a company are in the form of debts (receivables), the rules of sale of debt are applied on trading of its shares. On the contrary, if the assets of a company consist of goods, usufructs, rights,[5] cash and debts,[6] then the ruling of acquiring and trading shares of the company depends on the primary asset. The primary asset is the one which conforms to the main objective and business activity of the company. Therefore, in order for the trading of shares of a company to be allowed, it has to meet two conditions:

1. The primary asset should be illiquid; it means it has to be other than cash and debts;
2. And the value of the primary asset should not be less than 30% of the value of total assets of the company.

Comparatively, the criterion of ASIIP does not deal with the first condition, but it does include the second condition with a relaxed number as it allows the illiquid assets to decrease even until 25% of the total assets. However, the conceptual basis for this filter is same; this filter is applied to ensure that the illiquid assets would remain in a notable amount and would not become insignificant as compared to the liquid assets. This condition is employed because if all the assets are in liquid form and the shares are traded at any price other than their par value, then it would be tantamount to *riba* (Usmani 2011). This filter would ascertain that share trading would not become a means of dealing in currency exchange and sale of debt and hence avoid attracting the *Shariah* rulings of currency exchange and sale of debt for trading shares. This filter will be further discussed with the second filter of tradability later in this paper.

3.6 Net Liquid Assets/Share Vs Market Price/Share

According to PSX (2015a), it is a requirement that the market price per share should be equal to or greater than the net liquid assets per share. Net liquid assets per share is calculated by subtracting illiquid assets, current and long-term liabilities from total assets and divided by total number of shares outstanding.

This filter is actually related to the pervious filter of illiquid assets to total assets. According to PSX (2015a), since the trade price of liquid assets cannot deviate from their par value, those assets have to be traded for equal value in price. However, the illiquid assets can be traded for any price. Accordingly, this filter of (net liquid assets/share) versus (market price/share) basically ensures that there must be a portion in the price of shares which would be exactly equal to the value of liquid assets, while the remaining portion in price would be against the illiquid assets. In this way, the first filter of tradability ensures that the illiquid assets are in a considerable amount (25% of the total assets in the case of ASIIP) and shares do not merely represent liquid assets, whereas the second filter of tradability warrants that the liquid assets are traded at par value.

It seems that these two filters are based on the understanding that a share merely represents the assets of a company and its trading refers to merely exchanging those assets. These filters are derived through *ijtihad* from the classical *Fiqhi* issue of selling a *ribawi*[7] item mixed with a non-*ribawi* item for a price in the form of same *ribawi* item. This classical *Fiqhi* issue is based on a hadith and on its interpretation given by the Hanafi scholars. The hadith is stated as follows:

> Fudhalah Bin `Ubaid (R.A.) reported: I bought on the day (of the Victory of Khyber) a necklace for twelve dinars (gold coins). It was made

> of gold studded with gems. I separated (gold from gems) in it, and found (gold) of more (worth) than twelve dinars. I made a mention of it to Allah's Apostle (صلى الله عليه وسلم), whereupon he said: It should not be sold unless it is separated. (Muslim, n.d., hadith # 1591)

The hadith portrays a case of sale of a necklace that consisted of gold and gems for gold money (12 dinars). After the sale, the companion of the Prophet (صلى الله عليه وسلم) found that the amount of gold in the necklace was more than the amount of gold in 12 dinars. So the gold was not exchanged at par value. It was a spot sale, where *ribawi* item (gold) was combined with a non-*ribawi* item (gems) and sold for the same *ribawi* item (gold). There was no involvement of sale of debt or delayed payment of price. Hanafi scholars hold that the ruling of disallowing the sale in the above hadith was due to the fact that the exact amount of gold in the necklace was unknown. Moreover, it was later found that the gold price (12 dinars) was lesser than the amount of gold in the necklace, so equality in exchanging the same genus was also not observed (Usmani and Usmani 2006). However, such sale is allowed if it meets the following conditions:

1. Since such sale involves exchange of *ribawi* items of the same genus from both sides, mutual possession of the subject matter by both parties is required within the contract session.
2. The exact amount of *ribawi* items from both sides should be known.
3. The non-*ribawi* item that is mixed with the *ribawi* item should have some value and that value should not be small to the extent of negligibility.
4. The amount of *ribawi* item in price should be more than the amount of *ribawi* item of the same genus mixed with non-*ribawi* item. For instance, the gold in price should be more than the gold mixed with the non-*ribawi* item, so that the gold on both sides of the transaction would be exchanged at par and the remaining gold in price would be considered for the non-*ribawi* item. However, if the gold in price is less than or equal to the gold mixed with the non-*ribawi* item, then the sale is not allowed due to the presence of *riba* (Al-Kasani

Table 2 Examples of selling mixed *Ribawi* object and their *Shariah* rulings

No.	Price (*Ribawi*)	Object of sale (*Ribawi* + non-*Ribawi* item)		*Shariah* rulings
1	100 USD	1 kg dates	90 USD	Allowed (90 USD for 90 USD; remaining 10 USD for 1 kg dates)
2	90 USD	1 kg dates	90 USD	Not allowed (90 USD for 90 USD; 0 for 1 kg dates, *riba*!)
3	80 USD	1 kg date	90 USD	Not allowed (80 USD for 80 USD; 0 for 1 kg Dates and 10 USD, *riba*!)
4	80 USD + 1 kg dates	1 kg dates	90 USD	Allowed (80 USD for 1 kg dates; 90 USD for 1 kg dates)

Source Author's own

1986; Ibn Abidin 1992; Al-Sarakhsi 1993; Abu Zaid 2004; Usmani 2015b).

It can be made clearer with an example which is given in Table 2 below.

It is clear that the first filter of tradability in the ASIIP is based on the third condition mentioned above, whereas the second filter is based on the fourth condition. The connection between the case of an object made up of *ribawi* and non-*ribawi* items and the case of shares is that similar to the mixed object, shares also represent the assets that are a mixture of *ribawi* (liquid) and non-*ribawi* (illiquid) items. However, it is argued that as far as the exchange of an object consisting of *ribawi* and non-*ribawi* items (as in the case of exchanging gold necklace studded with gems for gold money) is concerned, the Hanafi approach seems to be valid. Nonetheless, there is a vast difference between a share of a company and a mere object consisting of *ribawi* and non-*ribawi* items.

A share of a company, more importantly, represents the company itself, its main business activities, human management, ability to produce and future prospects of generating revenues (Aal Sheikh 1979; Al-Manea 1996; Al-Qurahdaghi 2003). It is indeed more than a mere representation of the assets of a company. In fact, the representation of assets of the company by its share is a much controversial concept and weak point. According to Manjoo (n.d.), due to a great historical evolution in the concept of corporations and their shares, shares no longer represent the ownership of the assets of a company, rather they represent a bundle of rights that belong to the shareholders of a company. In support of his argument, he mentioned some real cases, like Macaura Vs Northern Assurance Co. Ltd (1925, AC 619) and R Vs Philippou (1989 89 Cr App R 290). Goulding (1996) also argued that a shareholder in a company does not own a "share" in the property of the company from the legal perspective. A company's property is legally owned by the company itself. Likewise, Abbasi (2009) and El-Gari (1998, 2015) iterated the same argument by mentioning that the property of a company cannot be attributed as the property of its shareholders in legal theory, just as the liabilities of a company cannot be attributed to the liabilities of its shareholders. Whether or not these opinions are to be taken at their face value, at least, they are sufficient to prove that the concept of shares merely representing the assets of a company is very contentious.

Secondly, the Hanafi scholars deem the sale of gold necklace studded with gems for gold price as currency exchange (*bay` al-sarf*). That is why they tend to apply the *Shariah* rulings of currency exchange in such sale. If shares, representing liquid and illiquid assets, are to be deemed as similar, then their trading should also be subject to the *Shariah* rulings of currency exchange. In other words, the first two conditions mentioned by the classical Hanafi scholars for such sale should also be observed. Employing those two conditions in acquiring and trading shares would mean that credit sale of shares would not be allowed. The shares and price both would have to be delivered within the contract session. And it would be necessary to exactly know the composition of assets of shares in terms of liquid and illiquid assets every time they are exchanged. These two conditions are not mentioned in the criterion of

ASIIP at all, and that is understandable because imposing such restrictions would definitely inflict a great challenge on share trading.

Thirdly, it is worth noting that the above-mentioned hadith and its interpretation by Hanafi scholars basically deal with the case of spot sale, where the object of sale is also a tangible asset and delivered on spot. Unlike that case, shares also represent receivables. Accordingly, selling shares mean that the receivables are sold to a third party along with other assets. In *Fiqh* literature, this situation is exactly same as the situation when a lender sells his debt, owed by a borrower, to a third party (other than the borrower). Such sale of debt to a third party is not allowed even at par value in Hanafi *Fiqh* (Al-Kasani 1986; Al-Sarakhsi 1993; Al-Nasafi 2011). So it is argued that if every type of asset represented by a share is separately taken into consideration, and given its own *Shariah* ruling, like cash and cash equivalent, would follow the rules of *bay` al-sarf*, illiquid assets would follow the rules of normal sale, then receivables should also follow their own ruling which demands that receivables should not be sold to a third party. This approach would definitely disallow the trading of shares according to Hanafi scholars.

On the contrary, Aal Sheikh (1979), Al-Manea (1996), Al-Qurahdaghi (2003), Al-Suwailem (2012), Al-Sanad (2012), Abu `Aliyu (2012) and many other scholars allow trading of shares without considering the condition of liquid and illiquid assets and their price as compared to the net liquid assets, because the assets are subsidiary in such transaction. In fact, SAC-SCM (2013) does not have any specific filter for liquidity in its criterion at all.

Therefore, in recognition of the conceptual confusion and practical difficulties, and knowing that a large group of scholars do not support the filter of tradability in share trading, it is proposed that the existence, role and necessity of such filters in the criterion of ASIIP should be re-examined. They can be even removed, because removing them would not only increase the theoretical clarity and confidence of the users of the criterion of ASIIP in its *Shariah* basis, but also avoid complications in employing the criterion. Furthermore, without these filters, it is believed that the universe of *Shariah* compliant companies in ASIIP would also expand, because many companies that are unable to pass the criterion due to these filters would be able to find their place in the list of *Shariah* compliant companies. Accordingly, the investors would be able to diversify their portfolio of equities to a greater extent. If it is feared that companies and investors would misuse the decision of removing the filters of tradability and take it as a way of dealing in currency and debt, then it can be decided on individual case basis. If it is found in an individual case that a company has become a vehicle for dealing in sale of currency and debt, it can be subject to a greater scrutiny, or consequently can be excluded from the list of ASIIP. However, it is not necessary that these filters should generally be employed on all companies.

4 A Proposal for Introducing a New Filter in the Screening Criterion

Under the compliance filters in the screening criterion of ASIIP, there are two filters to control a company's investment in impermissible ventures. The first filter is non-compliant income to total revenue, and the second filter is non-compliant investments to total assets. Consequently, if a company is involved in lending on interest by any means, not only there is a restriction on how much interest it can earn from the lending activity, but there is also a restriction on how much amount it can lend.

On the contrary, in order to control how much a company pays interest on its borrowing, there is only one filter which is interest-bearing debt to total assets. However, according to a hadith, paying interest is equally sinful as taking interest. It is narrated as follows:

> The Messenger of Allah (صلى الله عليه وسلم) cursed the accepter of interest and its payer, and one who records it, and the two witnesses, and he said: they are all equal (in guilt). (Muslim, n.d., hadith # 1598)

Therefore, for paying interest, a company should be restricted as much as it is restricted to take interest. Although Usmani (2015a, b) mention that the sin of making an interest-based contract and involving in it is same for the taker and payer of interest, taking interest can be more severe than paying interest in the sense that there is a factor of benefiting from something which is impermissible. That is why it is allowed to pay interest in a situation of dire need. Nevertheless, their argument does not necessitate that paying interest should always be perceived as lighter than taking interest. Moreover, since allowing to pay interest is a concession which is based on dire need, it should be exactly proportionate to the need itself.

In the context of screening criterion of ASIIP, the issue is not about whether or not to allow companies to pay interest, or whether or not there is a dire need to do so. The concession has already been made by allowing companies to involve in interest-bearing debt up to 37% of their total assets. Nonetheless, it is vital to gauge a filter that also restricts the interest payment itself. The issue is about constructing a more appropriate and robust filter that could exactly address the issue of impermissible element or activity and to give appropriate allowance to the companies and investors based on the established need.

It is interesting to notice that the filter of interest-bearing debt to total assets only puts a restriction on the amount of debt itself that a company has borrowed, but it does not put a restriction on the amount of interest it pays on the borrowed loan. In other words, the current filter addresses the issue of paying interest only in an indirect way. For example, if a company's interest-bearing debt is 36% of its total assets, it can easily pass the filter, without the concern that how much interest it actually pays on that debt. However, the main concern which provides the foundation of this filter is the payment of interest, not the amount of debt. The basic impermissible element that makes a transaction of loan on interest impermissible is *riba* (interest). The Holy Quran says as follows:

> God has allowed trade and forbidden usury. (Quran, Al-Baqarah 2:276, Translation by Abdul Haleem 2004)

> You who believe, beware of God: give up any outstanding dues from usury, if you are true believers. If you do not, then be warned of war from God and His Messenger. You shall have your capital if you repent, and without suffering loss or causing others to suffer loss. (Quran, Al-Baqarah 2:278–279, Translation by Abdul Haleem 2004)

This argument is also supported by the statement of Usmani (2015b) who says that stipulation of interest in a loan contract is void; if it is stipulated, then the condition itself would become void without invalidating the loan contract. Since the condition of interest is considered as void, while the contract remains valid, the ownership of the borrower over the principal amount would be recognised by *Shariah*. As a result, the principal amount or debt would be permissible to be used by the borrower. However, it goes without saying that the lender and borrower for involving in such a severely sinful transaction would be held responsible. Therefore, the main issue of payment of interest by a company should not be ignored.

In view of that, there is a need for a filter that could directly cater for the issue of paying interest. Therefore, it is necessary that a filter should be added to the criterion of ASIIP for serving the purpose of controlling the amount of interest payment as well. The proposed filter is interest expense to total revenue. In an ideal situation, the interest expense of a company to be *Shariah* compliant should be 0% of its revenues; however, since due to the dire need of interest-bearing loan for corporations, it can be tolerable, but should be kept within a certain percentage limit of total revenue. It can be calculated as follows:

Interest Expense to Total Revenue: (Interest Expense/Total Revenue).

The logic behind this filter is that it would check that how much a company pays interest out of its total revenue and restrict such payment based on a specific benchmark. It is out of the scope of this paper to propose an exact percentage limit for this filter, but it is proposed that a comprehensive empirical research should be conducted to determine a maximum percentage limit for it based on the concept of removal of hardship and recognition of dire need.

It is believed that this new filter would not only directly address the issue of paying interest, but also greatly contribute in the overall robustness of the *Shariah* screening criterion of ASIIP. Furthermore, it would also make the criterion of ASIIP more comprehensive and noble.

5 Conclusion and Recommendations

Keeping in view the objective of further growth of ICM in Pakistan, it is vitally imperative to carefully consider critical success factors that could boost the market and evolve it into a wider and deeper segment of the global ICM. Such efforts would definitely help building the road-map for future of ICM in particular, and Islamic finance in general, in Pakistan.

The recent launch of ASIIP is one of the remarkable steps taken towards leveraging on those critical success factors. The *Shariah* screening criterion is the backbone of ASIIP which needs to be more vigorous and comprehensive. In order to do so, this paper critically analysed the criterion from a *Shariah* perspective and thoroughly investigated its *Fiqhi* basis.

This paper recommends that the percentage limits of the four filters under the compliance category in the criterion should be reassessed by conducting a meticulous empirical research, as the current benchmarks seem to be too liberal. Their limit should be genuinely justified on the basis of actual dire need. Moreover, it also recommends that the two filters of tradability (negotiability) can be removed. They do not only lead to further theoretical incongruity and practical complications, but also tremble the investors' confidence in the credibility of the criterion which might consequently result in hampering progression of the ICM within the country.

More importantly, this paper presents a proposal for introducing entirely a new filter in the criterion. It proposes that a filter of interest expense to total revenue should be included in the compliance category in order to cater for the purpose of controlling interest payment of a company. Currently, there is only one filter which indirectly restricts the interest payment of a company. This new filter not only directly deals with the issue, but also contributes to the overall vigour of the criterion.

Notes

1. OIC is the abbreviation of Organization of Islamic Cooperation.
2. "'Umum balwa" is a fiqhi terminology which refers to "*an unfavorable widespread situation affecting most people and is difficult to avoid.*" (SAC-SCM 2006, p. 123)
3. SAC-SCM (2013) also has a limit of 20% of the total revenue for the income from certain type of business activities, but for interest, gharar, gambling, impermissible products-based businesses, it has 5% limit.
4. BSE is the abbreviation of Bombay Stock Exchange.
5. According to the definition of PSX (2015a), goods, usufructs and rights are the assets whose price can deviate from their par value according to the principles of *Shariah*.
6. According to the definition of PSX (2015a), cash and receivables are the assets whose price cannot deviate from their par value according to the principles of *Shariah*.
7. The term "ribawi" here means anything on which strict Shariah rules are applied in exchanging it in order to avoid riba, except for receivables. The case of receivables will be discussed separately.

References

Aal Al-Sheikh, M. (1979). *Fatāwā Wa Rasail*. Riyadh: The Government of Saudi Arabia.

Aal Sulaiman, M. (2006). *Al-Iktitab Wa Al-Mutajirah Bi Al-Ashum*. Riyadh: Dar Kunuz Eshbelia Li Al-Nashr Wa Al-Tauzee`.

AAOIFI. (2015). *Shari'a standards for Islamic financial institutions*. Manama: Accounting and Auditing Organization for Islamic Financial Institutions.

Abbasi, M. Z. (2009). Legal analysis of agency theory: An inquiry into the nature of corporation. *International Journal of Law and Management, 51*(6), 401–420.

Abdul Haleem, M. A. S. (2004). *The Qur'an*. New York: Oxford University Press Inc.

Abu 'Aliyu, A. A. A. (2012). *Tadawul Al-Ashum Wa Al-Ṣukūk Wa Dhawabit Al-Shar'iyyah*. Paper presented at the 20th discussion of International Islamic *Fiqh* Academy, Oran.

Abu Zaid, A. A. J. (2004). *Fiqh Al-Riba: Dirasah Muqaranah Wa Shamilah Li Al-Tatbiqat Al-Mu`asarah*. Damascus: Mu`assasah Al-Resalah.

Al-Bukhari, A. M. (2001). *Sahih Al-Bukhari*. Beirut: Dar Tauq Al-Nijah.

Al-Kasani, A. A. (1986). *Badā'i' Al-Ṣanā'i' Fi Tartib Al-Shara`i* (Vol. 2). Beirut: Dar al-Kotob al-Ilmiyah.

Al-Manea, A. (1996). *Buhuth Fi Al-Iqtisad Al-Islami*. Beirut: Al-Maktab Al-Islami.

Al-Nadwi, A. (2006). *Qa'idah Al-Taba'yyah Fi Al-`Uqud Wa Atharuha Fi Al-Tarakhusaat Al-Shar`iyyah*. In 1st *Fiqh* conference for Islamic finance institutions (pp. 39–70). Kuwait: Shura Sharia Consultancy.

Al-Nasafi, A. (2011). *Kanz Al-Daqa`iq*. Medina: Dar Al-Basha`ir Al-Islamiyyah, Dar Al-Siraj.

Al-Qurahdaghi, A. (2003). *Athar Duyun Wa Nuqud Al-Sharikah Aw Al-Mihfazhah 'Ala Hukm Tadawul Al-Ashum Wa Al-Ṣukūk Wa Al-Wahdat Al-Istithmāriyyah (Al-Wa Al-Hulul) – Dirasah Fiqhiyyah Iqtisaadiyyah* (Vol. 1). Jeddah: Islamic Institute for Research and Training (IIRT), Islamic Development Bank (IDB).

Al-Sanad, A. A. (2012). *Hukm Tadawul Al-Ashum Wa Al-Ṣukūk Wa Dhawabit Al-Shar'iyyah Ma' Bayan Dhabit Al-Taba'yyah Wa Shurutih Wa Waqt Tahakkuk Dhabit Al-Ghlabah Wa Shurutih*. Paper presented at the 20th Discussion International Islamic *Fiqh* Academy, Oran.

Al-Sarakhsi, S. (1993). *Al-Mabsūṭ*. Beirut: Dar Al-Marefah.

Al-Shubily, Y. (2015). *Al-Tauseef Al-Shar`I Li Al-Ashum Wa Al-Athaar Al-Mutarattibah `Alaih*. Paper presented at 6th Shura *Fiqh* conference, November 16–17, 2015, Salmiya, Kuwait.

Al-Suwailem, S. (2012). *Qawa'id Al-Ghalabah Wa Al-Taba'yyah Fi Al-Mu'amlat Al-Maliyyah Wa Tatbieqatiha Fi Tadawul Al-Ashum Wa Al- Wahdat Wa Al-Ṣukūk*. Paper presented at the 20th discussion International Islamic *Fiqh* Academy, Oran.

Al-Yahya, F. (2007). *Al-Mudharabah Ala Al-Ashum Qabl Bad`I Al-Sharikah Fi Nishatiha*. Paper presented at 15th international annual conference on securities markets & bourses prospects & challenges, 6–8 March 2007, Dubai, UAE.

Al-Zuhayli, M. M. (2006). *Al-Qawa'id Al-Fiqhiyyah Wa Tatbieqaatuhaa Fi Al-Mathaahib Al-Arba'a* (Vol. 1). Damascus: Dar Al-Fikr.

DJIMI. (2015). *Dow Jones Islamic market indices methodology*. Available at: https://www.djindexes.com/mdsidx/downloads/meth_info/Dow_Jones_Islamic_Market_Indices_Methodology.pdf.

El-Gari, M. A. (1998). Al-Shakhsiyyah Al-I'tibariyyah That Al-Masuliyyah Al-Mahdoudah. *Islamic Economic Studies, 5*(2), 3–15.

El-Gari, M. A. (2015). *Al-Takyīf Al-Fiqhī Li Ashum Sharikat Al-Musahamah.* Paper presented at 6th Shura *Fiqh* conference, November 16–17, 2015, Salmiya, Kuwait.

FTSE. (2015). *Ground rules for the FTSE Sharī'ah global equity index series.* FTSE version 2.2, December 2015. Available at: http://www.ftse.com/products/downloads/FTSE_Sharī'ah_Global_Equity_Index_Series.pdf.

Goulding, S. (1996). *Principles of company law.* London, UK: Cavendish Publishing Limited.

Hassan, H. H. (2015). *Al-Takyīf Al-Fiqhī Li Ashum Sharikat Al-Musahamah.* Paper presented at 6th Shura *Fiqh* conference, November 16–17, 2015, Salmiya, Kuwait.

Ibn Abidin, M. A. (1992). *Radd Al-Muḥtār 'ala Al-Durr Al-Mukhtar.* Beirut: Dar Al-Fikr.

IFSB. (2016). *Islamic Financial Services Industry Stability Report.* Kuala Lumpur: Islamic Financial Services Board (IFSB).

Khatkhatay, M. H., & Nisar, S. (2007). Shariah compliant equity investment: An assessment of current screening norms. *Islamic Economic Studies, 15*(1), 47–76.

Maghrebi, N., & Mirakhor, A. (2015). Risk sharing and shared prosperity in Islamic finance. *Islamic Economic Studies, 23*(2), 85–115. http://doi.org/10.12816/0015201.

Manjoo, F. A. (n.d.). *Reviewing the concept of shares: Towards a dynamic legal perspective.* Available at: http://www.kantakji.com/media/163525/file519.pdf.

Mansoori, M. T., & Khan, A. (2015). Investment in equities: Sharī'ah appraisal of screening norms. *Journal of Islamic Business and Management, 5*(1), 51–68.

MSCI. (2015). *MSCI Islamic index series methodology.* Available at: https://www.msci.com/eqb/methodology/meth_docs/MSCI_April15_Islamic_Indexes_Methodology.pdf.

Muslim, (n.d.). *Sahih Muslim.* Beirut: Dar Ihya Al-Turath al-Arabi.

PSX. (2015a). *All shares Islamic index of Pakistan brochure.* Karachi: PSX. Available at: https://www.psx.com.pk/scripts/communicator.php?f=AllShrIslamic_Idx_Brochure.pdf&l=tXt.

PSX. (2015b). *KMI—30 index brochure*. Karachi: PSX. Available at: https://www.psx.com.pk/scripts/communicator.php?f=BrochureKMI_Idx.pdf&l=tXt.

S&P. (2015). *S&P Dow Jones Shariah indices methodology*. October, 2015. Available at: https://us.spindices.com/documents/methodologies/methodology-sp-*Shariah*-indices.pdf?force_download=true.

SAC-SCM. (2006). *Resolutions of the securities commission Sharīʿah advisory council*. Kuala Lumpur: Securities Commission Malaysia.

SAC-SCM. (2013). *Frequently-asked questions on revised Sharīʿah screening methodology*. Available at: http://www.sc.com.my/frequently-asked-questions-on-revised-Sharīʿah-screening-methodology/.

Usmani, M. I. A. (2015a). *Islamic finance*. Karachi: Quranic Publishers.

Usmani, M. T. (2007). *Islam or Jadeed Ma`ishat Wa Tijarat*. Karachi: Maktabah Mariful Quran.

Usmani, M. T. (2011). *Fiqhī Maqalaat*. Karachi: Memon Islamic Publishers.

Usmani, M. T. (2015b). *Fiqh Al-Buyūʿ ʿala Al-Madhahib Al-Arba`ah*. Karachi: Quranic Studies Publishers.

Usmani, S. A., & Usmani, M. T. (2006). *Mawsūʿah Fath Al-Mulhim Bi Sharḥ Sahih Al-Imam Muslim*. Beirut: Dar Ihya Al-Turath Al-Arabi.

Introducing Islamic Finance in Unchartered Economies: The Case of Canada

Baharom Abdul Hamid, Mohsin Ali, Wajahat Azmi and Zaheer Anwer

Abstract The primary goal of this paper is to explore the viability of initiating Islamic finance (IF) in an unchartered economy. Canada is taken as a case study for this paper. To achieve our objective, we proceed in two stages. The first stage involves the analysis of market opportunities for IF. More precisely, the first stage involves the cost/benefit analysis which would enable the IF industry to see whether it is feasible for them to initiate. Second, the more challenging stage involves the analysis with regard to the barriers in offering IF products. In other words, we examine whether some of the IF products can be offered in the current regulatory framework. More importantly, we also examined the current banking regulations, which might hinder the offering of IF products, and provide suggestions on the amendments that can be made to ensure the smooth start. Broadly speaking, in this paper, we dispel certain myths surrounding the system such as it is not compatible with the contemporary finance and Muslims exclusivity etc. Based on the

B.A. Hamid (✉) · M. Ali · W. Azmi · Z. Anwer
INCEIF, Kuala Lumpur, Malaysia
e-mail: baharom@inceif.org

S.A.R. Rizvi and I. Saba (eds.), *Developments in Islamic Finance*, Palgrave CIBFR Studies in Islamic Finance, DOI 10.1007/978-3-319-59342-5_6

demography, established ethical market, existence of Islamic indices and the mutual funds, and its high rank in the Islamicity index, we argue that Canada could be one of the avenues to initiate Islamic financial system. We have also highlighted some of the economic benefits of such system in terms of its impact on economic growth. Additionally, we have also elaborated on how its risk-sharing characteristic and attachment to real economy could be beneficial for Canadian economy in terms of lowering the risk of banking crises and stock market crashes.

Keywords Islamic finance · Unchartered economy · Developed countries

1 Introduction

The recent financial turmoil of 2007–2008 has once again highlighted the vulnerabilities of conventional financial system. The conventional financial system was presumed to be superior to the non-interest system on the grounds of efficiency and stability (Chapra 2007). However, the long lists of crises that have happened over the years have weakened the arguments. As per Stiglitz (2003), the number of crises that have happened over the last four decades is more than 100. Time and again, this inherent weaknesses of conventional financial system has forced the policymakers to look for a more robust, resilient, and sustainable financial system. In that sense, Islamic financial system is seen as a viable alternative to a current system. The main source of resilience and stability of this system comes from its detachment from the interest-based structure and reliance on risk-sharing principles.

The Second Strategic Roundtable Discussion, jointly organized by the International Shariah Research Academy for Islamic Finance (ISRA), the Islamic Research and Training Institute (IRTI), and Durham University, met on September 20, 2012, in Lanai Kijang, Kuala Lumpur, and issued what is known as the Kuala Lumpur Declaration whereby after lengthy deliberations on the issue of risk sharing, the participants acknowledged that the financial crisis which started in 2008 highlighted the fact that the most salient feature of the dominant conventional financial system is the transfer of risks away from financial institutions onto customers, governments, and the public at large. IF is in a unique position to offer an alternative to the present interest-based debt financing regime that has brought the whole world to the edge of collapse. Bearing this in mind, the second annual ISRA-IRTI-Durham Strategic Roundtable Discussion (2012) agreed that the Shariah emphasizes risk sharing as a salient characteristic of Islamic financial transactions.

One of the popular misconceptions that most of the people have is that risk sharing is something new; on the contrary, risk sharing had been practiced quite long ago. In fact, the first industrial revolution is generally agreed to have taken place in 1784–1870, whereby the revolution is characterized by the use of water and steam power, new infrastructure development, transportation evolution, mechanization of production, factories, and railways, and it was influenced by the school of thought of Adam Smith, whereby the community and the society matters, risk-sharing financial model was applied. It was even carried thru to the second industrial revolution. Only the third industrial revolution (1950–1990) is the era of computers, rapid advance of computing, digital automation of production, advances in space travel, and massive technological payoffs, whereby heavily influenced by the schools of neoclassical and neoliberalism and the tenet was there is no such a thing as a society, it is only collection of individuals, thus risk transfer and risk shifting rules.

Although IF is still in its infancy stage, especially in the Western countries, it is gaining prominence and acceptance all over the world much faster. Based on the recent growth trends, the future prospects of Islamic financial industry seem promising. The possibility of bright prospects gets reaffirmed with the regulatory developments concerning the Islamic banking sector in uncharted countries, especially by the conventional financial centers.[1]

The primary goal of this paper is to explore the viability of initiating Islamic finance in an uncharted economy. Canada is taken as a case study for this paper.

Following are the several reasons for selecting Canada as a case study:

(a) Demographics

- Canada is generally viewed as one of the technologically advanced countries.
- It has a significant population of Muslims, numbers currently believed to be 1 million.
- The Muslims in Canada are viewed as being more educated than the average Canadian.

(b) Lack of Islamophobia

- Canada has proven to house a more open society in terms of accepting people from different faith, background, race, etc.
- Canada took the highest number of Syrian refugees among the non-Islamic countries.

(c) Prerequisite Islamic characteristics

- Canada seems to be more Islamic than any of the Islamic countries (in fact, it is ranked 13th in Islamicity index).

(d) Developed ethical market

- Canada is definitely one of the leading countries in terms of ethical/responsible/sustainable investing, and there is also presence of Islamic indices (Dow Jones, MSCI, etc.).

More briefly, we answer the question: Can Canada and IF benefit from each other? To achieve the objective, we explore several avenues on how Canada can benefit from IF and vice versa. More precisely, we outline the exclusive offerings of IF, especially in terms of unique risk-sharing characteristics and its closeness to real economy. Moreover, we also provide the economic benefits of IF in terms of its impact on economic growth and other macroeconomic factors. Furthermore, we also highlight the Islamic finance solutions to the problems faced by the conventional financial system.

2 What Is Islamic Finance?

Islam is not only a religion, but a complete code of life. Quran and the life traditions of the Prophet Muhammad (pbuh) provide us a blueprint for daily life. From family dealings and marriage to permissible edibles, and from modest dress sense and fineness in social manners to ethics in commerce and finance, Islam embraces all facets of our existence. One such facet is "Islamic finance" which is expanding rapidly and gathering interest from not only Muslims but also non-Muslim communities as well.

IF refers to financial transactions conforming to Islamic Jurisprudence (Sharia Law). Islamic Jurisprudence generally applies negative screening in the cases of Muamalat. There are a number of screenings applied in Islamic finance as well. One of the main screens is the prohibition of riba (interest) in a financial transaction. Riba refers to all forms of interest and is not limited to usury or excessive interest only. In Islamic finance, money is only considered as a medium of exchange and not recognized as a commodity. Hence, any return purely on money is prohibited, and returns are required to be tied to an asset, or participation and risk taking in a joint venture.

In Islamic finance, the alternates to a pure debt security are "asset-based" security, real asset financing, and different forms of partnerships. Debt-based transactions where underlying subject matter is an asset are permissible. In addition to impermissibility of riba, there are few other major screenings that are also required to be passed by a financial transaction to be termed as Islamic. These include the prohibition of gharar, maisir, hoarding, as well as trading in prohibited commodities, for example, pork and alcohol.

3 Is It Only for Muslims?

Due to the word Islam in the name of the term "Islamic Finance," novices may get an impression that it is for Islamic world only. This is a misconception and is required to be addressed loudly to make sure that it does not hamper the growth of Islamic finance in non-Muslim majority countries like Canada. There is no prohibition on the use of Islamic financial products by non-Muslims; on the contrary, many conventional banking groups such as Citigroup, HSBC, and Standard Chartered, among others, are already offering Islamic financial services.

As far as prohibitions enforced by Shariah law against usury, investments in sectors such as alcohol, gambling, and pornography are concerned; other major world religions including Christianity, Judaism, Buddhism, and Hinduism also impose similar restriction. As for as Canada is concerned, 68% of the population is identified as Christian. Bible, which is followed by almost all the Christians and Jews, has several injunctions which prohibit the act of giving and collection of interest. Several passages in the Old Testament condemn usury, one of which is Deuteronomy 23:19–20

> You shall not charge interest on loans to your brother, interest on money, interest on food, interest on anything that is lent for interest. You may charge a foreigner interest, but you may not charge your brother interest, that the Lord your God may bless you in all that you undertake in the land that you are entering to take possession of it.

This led to lending money on interest banned in the Jewish community, but it was allowed to outsiders. But medieval Roman Catholic Church reinterpreted the above-mentioned passage. As per Dr. Alastair McIntosh from the Centre for Human Ecology, "Christianity extended the view of God's people to all of human kind, it meant not just not lending within your community, but also not lending full stop, at any rate of interest".[2] A passage in the Gospels Luke 6: 34–35 reports Jesus as saying the following:

> And if you lend to those from whom you expect repayment, what credit is that to you? Even sinners lend to sinners, expecting to be repaid in full. But love your enemies, do good to them, and lend to them without expecting to get anything back. Then your reward will be great, and you will be children of the Most High, because he is kind to the ungrateful and wicked. that those who lend should not expect anything in return.

In addition to that, IF was also featured in the Vatican's official newspaper, Osservatore Romano, which stated that "The ethical principles on which IF is based may bring banks closer to their clients and to the true spirit which should mark every financial service." It shows the acceptability of IF in the wider territories.

For non-Muslims, IF is to be considered as an alternative to conventional mode of financial transaction which follows a distinct set of values and bounds. In addition to that, IF is supposed to make commercial sense, as otherwise it would be improbable that any individual chooses it over its counterpart.

4 Literature Review

IF industry is almost three decades old now, and there are different empirical studies made with the intention to assess the impact of IF on various economic indicators and banking system. In this pursuit, Čihák and Hesse (2008) assessed 18 banking systems having dual banking systems in order to evaluate relative financial strength of IBs. They found small IBs to be financially stronger as compared to small commercial banks and large IBs, whereas large commercial banks were financially stronger than large IBs. They found that IBs did not affect the soundness of other banks in a country's financial system. IBs had higher exposure to risk that may be compensated by higher returns.

Imam and Kpodar (2015) analyzed the impact of IB development on macroeconomic growth for a sample of 52 developing economies (29 OIC countries) for the period 1990–2010. They observed that even though the size of IB was relatively small as compared to the economy and the overall financial system, IB was positively associated with economic growth. IB was also found responsive to the specific unmet needs of households and firms. IB did not appear to crowd out traditional finance and is expected to complement conventional banking rather than substituting it. Finally, countries with IB experienced faster economic growth than others.

Al-Fawwaz et al. (2015) used a sample of Jordan Islamic Bank and showed that IF had positive relationship with GDP and domestic investment and negative correlation with inflation. Besides, expansion of IF plays an important part in boosting GDP and removing weakness of the domestic investment. It also enhances the pace of growth of the economy.

Gheeraert and Weill (2015) studied 70 countries from Middle East and Southeast Asia for the period 2000–2005 and found that development of IB favors efficiency, and it is not an obstacle to aggregate productivity.

Even though these studies build a strong case in support of IF, the evidence is inconclusive mainly due to the reason that IF is not very old and it requires more time to assess its impact on economy and banking system with more reliability.

5 IF—Current Scenario[3]

IF has experienced notable growth in the course of last decade as is evident from the industry figures. Islamic banking assets stood at USD 660 billion in 2008 that swelled to more than USD 1515 billion in 2014. At present, GCC and MENA regions are the main drivers of this growth, but a prominent number of IB assets (USD 200 Billion) are outstanding in other Asian Markets as well. IF has achieved an average CAGR of 16% in assets, financing, and deposits during the period 2008–2013, and except some little variation, this trend is persistent since 2008. The average ROA for investors is 1% and average ROE is 2.3% that should be interpreted keeping in view the fact that IF offers more stability, so the returns may be lower than the market. The growth of Sukuk industry is another milestone for IF that has achieved CAGR of 20.78% for the period 2008–2013 and rose as high as USD 310 billion in 2014. It is therefore no surprise that the markets where both IBs and conventional banks (CBs) coexist, IBs have shown much higher growth as compared to CBs in terms of key variables (Fig. 1).

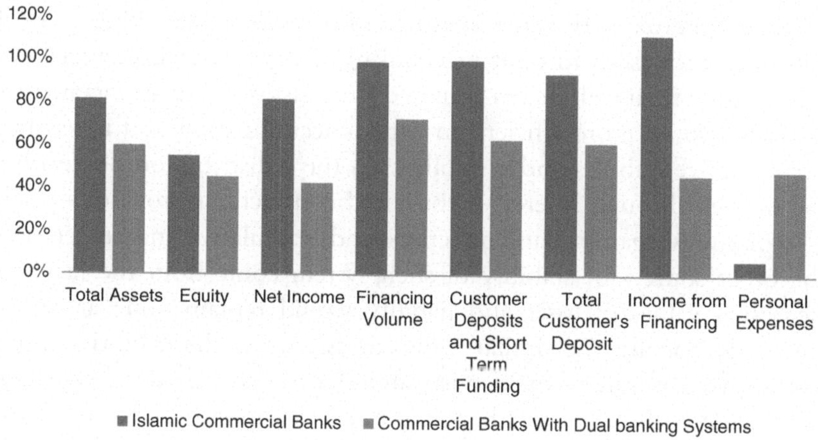

Fig. 1 Islamic banking versus commercial banking (% growth of selected variables)

6 What Does iF Offers?

6.1 Real Economy

As Islam encompasses all the aspects of life, it is not surprising that it covers one of the most important aspects, i.e., finance. Islam provides the detailed outline about the finance/investment decision-making. Following these guidelines, one would realize that Islamic finance is very comprehensive and is much more than a mere financial contract. Based on its comprehensiveness, it is often projected as an alternative financial system. More importantly, it is not exclusively for Muslims, but for all. Secondly, it puts the financial services to more productive and efficient use as it links the financial services to real economy.

On the one hand, we have real sector which is related to production of goods and services through use of factors of production, while on the other hand, we have financial sector which is there to facilitate the funding of this produce through intermediation. One of the fundamental flaws with the current financial system is that it has moved far away from the real sector which has resulted in many crises over the years. Islamic financial system provides a perfect solution to this issue as it brings financial sector more close to real sector.

The main crux of IF is risk sharing as opposed to risk taking and risk shifting, which is an in-built mechanism of conventional financial system. Islamic financial system founded on a risk-sharing arrangement is advocated to be more efficient in capital accumulation and is resistant to speculative bubbles and instability. As the redistribution of wealth is not allowed through interest-/debt-based contracts, it provides a shield to economies against banking crises and speculative market crashes. The other sources of stability of such system come from the fact that the actual values of asset and liability would remain same at all the time. Additionally, the similar values of assets and the liabilities would ensure that the return on deposit and the investment do not diverge much from each other, and hence, the real sector and the financial sector would be closely tied to each other. Moreover, the close relationship would also imply that the return on financial sector is dependent on the real sector and not the other way around. The system based on such characteristics is deemed to be capable of creating more employment, income, and growth (Askari et al. 2010). At one end of the spectrum, sales and purchases of already produced goods would be facilitated in order to allow greater production and hence greater employment of resources. On the other end, funding for the planned future production would be provided, and this would be done via risk-sharing arrangements (Mirakhor 2010). Naturally, there is no room for purely financial transactions in such a system (Mirakhor 2012).

6.2 Risk Sharing

[4]As the external environment is a set of controllable and uncontrollable factors, risk and uncertainty stand as essential features of business. It is not possible, beyond a reasonable limit, to predict future, and therefore, investment outcomes are forward-looking. Evidently, predetermination of interest rate is unjustified as the fixation is made irrespective of the business results and property rights are not properly transferred to the lender(s). IF, as an alternative, offers "risk sharing" which is a consistent mechanism for distribution of risk and reward in which property rights are exchanged in an equitable manner in order to allow both the parties to

share production, transportation, as well as marketing risks (Askari 2012). The parties are bound by a contract to share and effectively reduce the risk of income volatility that is otherwise multiplied in case of conventional devices like risk transfer and risk shifting. In this manner, this approach produces a stronger linkage between financial sector and real sector.

The exchange process facilitates risk taking in real economy as no party is overburdened. Islam permits this exchange, and IF has introduced partnership-based risk-sharing agreements (like Mudarabah and Musharakah) in light of Shariah rulings. In addition to contracts made at individual or group levels, equity markets emerge as an ideal platform for practicing these contracts at the institutional level. The role of governments is critical in this respect because a fair distribution of property rights cannot be materialized without the effective governance. IF can be viewed as a constant pursuit of sustainability, and risk-sharing philosophy is instrumental in the achievement of this goal as it enhances the capacity of society to absorb adverse shocks.

6.3 Institutional Structure

In order to promote IF and reap its desired benefits, wealth creation has to be made in line with risk-sharing principle, and redistribution measures, as stipulated by Shariah, have to be adopted. Islam does not forbid from earning wealth, and protection of wealth is even among objectives of Shariah. However, there should be no element of oppression (zulm) involved, and the ownership interests and property rights should be protected. IF devises both sales-based and equity-based contracts and endeavor to promote fair markets to practice these contracts. The ultimate objective is seeking morality and economic justice through fostering an "ethical" open economy where participants exhibit values of trust and mutuality.

6.4 IF Solution to Conventional Banking Problems

Conventional banking possesses inherent weaknesses as it is based on wants and encourages their satisfaction, regardless of consequences.

Therefore, massive debt is issued with the help of money created through fractional reserve system, thereby forming artificial assets. This approach results in financial crisis like 1997 East Asia Crisis, 1998 Russia, 1999 Argentina, and 2008 Global Crisis, only to name a few. The regulations fail to stop these crises due to their inability to address the root cause and collusion between research and management. They are reactive in nature instead of being proactive.

Islamic teachings, on the other hand, believe in limiting desires and urge its followers to fulfill not only their own needs but also assist others in doing so. Thus, profit seeking is not the only desired motive of business for Muslims as they are required to redistribute their wealth through mandatory channel of Zakat and other voluntary channels like Charities and Waqf. Furthermore, ownership is a prerequisite of sale, and the transactions are linked to physical exchange of property resulting in the prevention of speculation. IF prohibits excessive risk taking and lack of transparency (gharar) that in many cases are essential elements of products developed through financial engineering. This arrangement contributes to long-term stability of the system and thus assists regulators in protecting the system.

6.5 IF Economic Benefits

In this section, we highlight the economic benefits of implementing Islamic finance. To do so, we draw parallels from QISMUT (Qatar, Indonesia, Saud Arabia, Malaysia, UAE, and Turkey) countries. We deliberately chose QISMUT countries as it is the fastest growing region in terms of Islamic finance. It is expected to lead the growth of Islamic finance in near future (Ernst and Young report 2016).[5] As per the report, approximately 93% of the total Islamic banking asset is based in 9 countries out of which 80% are in QISMUT countries. The most dominant country in this region is Saudi Arabia with ownership of more than 30% of total asset followed by Malaysia and UAE. It is evident from these statistics that QISMUT countries are important with respect to Islamic financial system. However, the dynamics of Canada is very different from these countries, but it still provides a ground for a good comparison.

In the above figure, green and red lines reveal the proportion of conventional banking and Islamic banking in the total banking asset, respectively. The blue line is the GDP growth of QISMUT countries. We can see the proportion of conventional banking asset to total banking asset is declining over the years.

In Fig. 2, we map the growth of Islamic and the conventional banking assets with GDP growth of QISMUT countries. It is evident from the graph that the GDP growth is more closely related to the growth of Islamic banking assets than the conventional banking assets. In fact, the growth of conventional banking asset is almost stagnant and low over the last few years.

The above Figs. 3 and 4 depict the GDP growth of Canada and QISMUT countries over the last decade. It is clear from the figure that

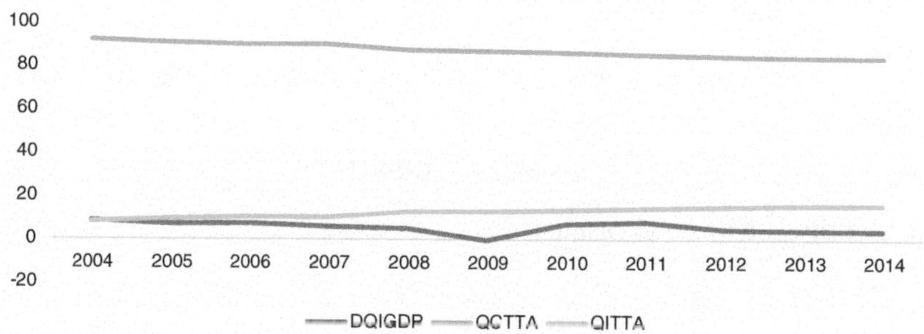

Fig. 2 Islamic banking, conventional banking, and GDP growth

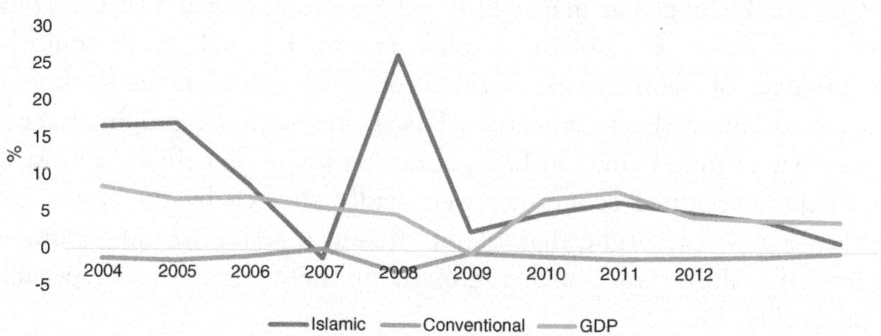

Fig. 3 Growth of conventional/Islamic banking asset and GDP

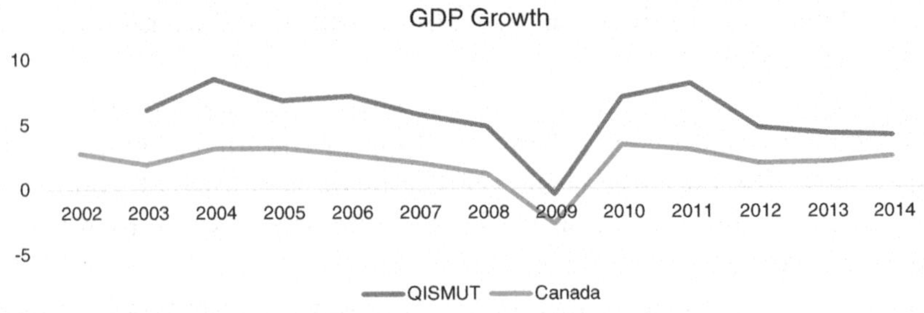

Fig. 4 GDP growth—QISMUT vs Canada

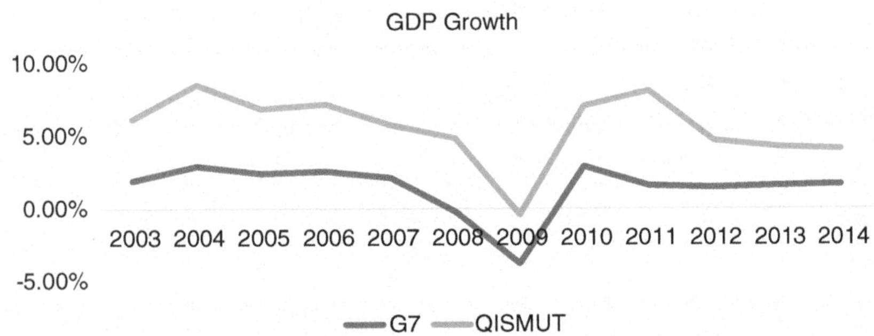

Fig. 5 GDP growth: G7 vs QISMUT

QISMUT has outperformed Canada in terms of its growth. The most striking highlight of above graph is the performance of these two during the crisis.

QISMUT somewhat managed to escape the impact of crisis as compared to Canada. One of the possible reasons for such result could be the presence of Islamic banks in these countries as Islamic banks showed great resistant to the recent crisis. Based on the above graphs, we can argue that Islamic banks do bring some economic benefits. As most of the major developed economies were badly affected by the recent crisis (see Fig. 4), we argue that Islamic financial system could become a source of stability and further growth of these economies, especially Canada (Fig. 5).

7 Why Canada?

7.1 Growth Drivers for Islamic Finance in Canada

Canadian economy possessing world's safest banking system is already host to IF industry owing to the presence of a significant number of Muslims who are currently 3% of the population and expected to be 6.6% approximately by 2030. Canada can be a great opportunity for the growth of IF owing to its competitiveness, ease of doing business, strong macroeconomic fundamentals, as well as its strategic location that links it with other important markets like USA, Asia, Europe, Africa, and the Middle East. In addition to this, Canada is endowed with natural resources as wealth ranging from mining to hydrocarbons. These factors jointly provide an ideal environment for Shariah compliant investors.

The familiarity level of Canadians regarding IF is very high owing to the decades-old Islamic mortgage finance in Canada initiated by Ansar Co-operative Housing Corporation. The availability of IF education through several tertiary education institutions like Centennial College (offering online courses) and other institutions like University of Toronto and McMaster University (offering an MBA-level Islamic finance course) has played an important role in enhancing this awareness. The government departments are also entering into transactions involving Shariah compliant contracts. For example, in 2014, Export Development Canada (EDC) disbursed a US$200 million Murabaha facility to Etihad Etisalat Company (Mobily).

IF has emerged as a niche industry in Canada, and its growth can be observed in various sectors. Islamic mortgage industry is exhibiting higher growth rate as compared to conventional mortgage industry. In a similar manner, Takaful industry that dates back to 2008 is also growing, and the Takaful solutions for home and auto products are being offered by leading insurance providers of Canada like The Co-operators Group and Sun Life. Islamic asset management is also progressing, and there are various Islamic funds in Canada including the Global Iman Fund and emerging players like AGInvest Properties Canada who are specialist in farmland investment. It is not difficult to gauge the depth and diversity of existing IF investment in Canada that has further prospects of expansion.

The global crisis and decreasing interest rates have been among the other motivating factors for IF industry as it offers risk-sharing contracts and a variety of avenues for investment that offer lucrative returns. The industry is widening, and there are opportunities available for cross-border investments. The increase in investment in global Sukuk is an indication of this trend.

Canadian IF industry also has the privilege to benefit from Islamic Finance Advisory Board (IFAB) that is an independent, non-profit organization. It provides professional and authoritative Shariah compliant advisory to the industries and individuals in order to improve awareness. It also provides financial services industry in Canada with Shariah audit functions, and the coverage includes financial institutions located in Ontario, Manitoba, and Alberta.

7.2 Challenges

In spite of the promising opportunities for IF industry in Canada, there are certain challenges that can restrict the progression of IF. These issues are not unique to the Canadian environment, and other jurisdictions are also experiencing these difficulties. The distinguished design of IF products can be cited as the core reason as the present financial system and past financial system are used to interest-based system, and there are certain constraints involved in their implementation.

To begin with, IF products pose a challenge from a tax perspective owing to the lack of knowledge on part of tax authorities and taxpayers regarding specific features of IF products. The users of IF products may need to pay more tax as compared to the other investors due to involvement of multiple contracts, and they may require significant resources to approach tax authorities and obtain favorable rulings. This process can linger on especially in the case of Muslim minority country like Canada where authorities do not possess adequate understanding of the exact nature of the product and its corresponding tax treatment. If Canada can address the taxation issue of IF industry, it can be predicted that more financial institutions will offer Shariah compliant products.

Another important issue is related to education and competent human resources of IF. There is a global shortage of experienced professionals in the IF industry, and Malaysia and Bahrain are among key providers of training, education, and professional development programs. This lack of skilled professionals can be a hurdle in the development of IF community in Canada. In this respect, Toronto Financial Services Alliance's Centre of Excellence in Financial Services Education can play an important role in ensuring the availability of relevant skills.

Finally, the regulatory framework in Canada has yet to develop regulations for dedicated Islamic banks owing to the distinguished nature of IF products and unique challenges associated with these instruments.

7.3 The Common Grounds

Similar to other developed countries, Social Responsible Investment's (SRI) share has increased rapidly in Canada. This is especially because of shift by institutional investors which is nearly 95% of the total assets under management that incorporates some form of responsible investment criteria. SRI and Islamic finance have been two of the most fast growing areas of finance in recent times. During the last couple of years, both of them have grown at faster rates than the financial markets as a whole.[6] According to estimates, the total volume of Islamic financial assets has grown by 15–20% a year and now exceeds USD1 tln, whereas in 2013, the total volume of assets held by explicitly SRI investors exceeded USD21.4 tln, having increased by more than 30% since 2005.[7] In both the cases, investors earned high returns on their investments. In addition, there are social returns to the society as well. Canada represents 4.4% of SRI market, but it has been growing rapidly.

Terms such as ethical, equitable, social, and sustainable investments are all identical to both Islamic finance and SRI. Furthermore, sustainability is also a key common factor between SRI and Islamic finance. There have been some efforts globally to integrate these commonalities. One such initiative is by SAM (Sustainable Asset Management), which is one of the leading asset managers in the field of sustainability investments and has ventured with a UK Islamic Bank, Gatehouse Bank, to come up with the first ever Shariah compliant water-focused investment strategy. There is room for more such initiatives in Canada where SRI has already been a success.

7.4 Forecasting—Islamic Finance in Canada

Currently, there are around 1.3 million Muslims living in Canada, which makes around 2.8% of the total population. As per Pew Research Center report called The Future of The Global Muslim, by 2030, the Muslim population will reach to about 2.7 million in Canada, which will be about 6.6% of the total population. As per the study, the number of Muslim consumers is growing faster in Canada than in the USA,[8] which suggests the expected increase in the demand for Islamic finance products. Here we discuss the expected growth trends of different categories of Islamic finance in Canada.

7.5 Sukuk

As discussed earlier, after implementing negative screening criteria, the main focus of Islamic finance is to conduct financial transactions which can be linked to the real economy. Islamic finance provides flexible structures to be used for asset-backed, based or project financing. Infrastructure development is considered as a vital ingredient to support and enhance economic growth. But similar to many countries,

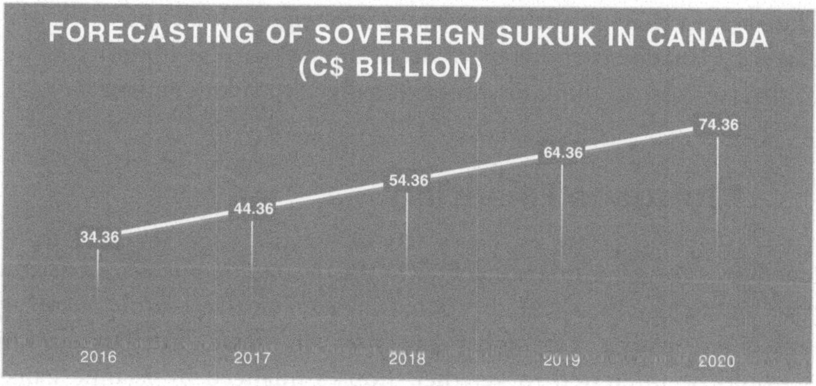

Fig. 6 Forecasting of sovereign sukuk in Canada

the infrastructure development sector has been underinvested in Canada as well mainly due to its long-term nature. As per the Canadian Infrastructure Report Card, the replacement cost of underdeveloped infrastructure is estimated to be C$171.8 billion, or 9% of GDP, based on its level at the end of 2015.[9]

One way to finance these infrastructure requirements could be by issuing shorter-tenor sovereign sukuk. These sukuk would be more appropriate for most of the infrastructure development projects like drinking water, wastewater, storm water system, and municipal roads, which do not have direct cash flows to support sukuk. These sukuk would be asset based in terms of structure, so that they do not carry a higher-risk weight than a project-based sukuk, which would make them interesting for Islamic bank as well.

For the purpose of forecasting, we assume that Canadian government plans to finance all the underinvested infrastructure projects amounting C$171.8 billion in next 5 years, and there would be an additional requirement of C$10 billion each year. We also assume that the government plans to finance 10% of the required amount by issuing sovereign sukuk, so that the investors and Islamic banks from oil-rich countries can be attracted (Fig. 6).

Further to the infrastructure-based sovereign sukuk, there are prospects for Canada's corporates to tap domestic Muslim liquidity as well as a diverse base of sukuk investors globally with sukuk issuance.

8 Mortgage Financing

Generally, mortgage financing makes up the major portion of Islamic retail financing. To assess the potential size of the Islamic mortgage market, we assume that most Muslims and few Christian customers would be interested to get their houses financed by Islamic banks. For Muslims, we use the projected population numbers from the Pew Research Center's 2010–2030 projections. To convert the Muslim population into household who would be considered as the home buying population, we divided the Muslim population of 1.3 million by the average household size of Canada, i.e., 2.5.[10] Similarly, we have divided Christian population of 22.10 million[11] by the average household size of Canada. For the population growth, we will extrapolate on the basis of data provided by PEW research center. In North America, the Christian population is expected to grow by 8% over the period of 2010–2050. So we will extrapolate to get the required data.

The average sales price of a house in Canada in 2016 is C$503,301,[12] which will be used in our estimate of Mortgage financing in Canada. These prices have a growth rate of 4.73%.[13] We assume that all home purchases will be made with a 20% down payment. As a rule of thumb, which is applied in the industry, about one-third of the Muslim population is not price sensitive and will prefer Islamic finance over its counterpart. Another 50–60% of Muslims will consider Islamic finance if it is cost competitive.[14] So to make it simpler, we assume that around 50% of the Muslims will avail the home financing from Islamic banks. As far as Christians are concerned, we assume that 10% of Christians will also prefer Islamic mortgage over other alternatives. We have also taken into consideration the fact that not all the population is going to apply for the house financing. We assume that 70% of the population would apply for home financing. The results are overwhelming and show interesting opportunities for big size banks of Canada. In 2016,

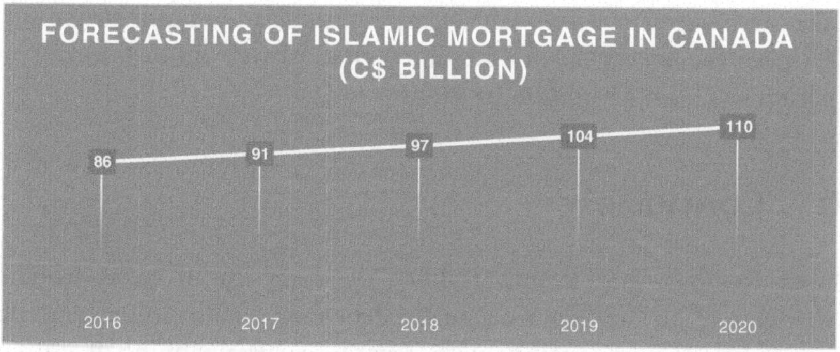

Fig. 7 Forecasting of Islamic mortgages in Canada

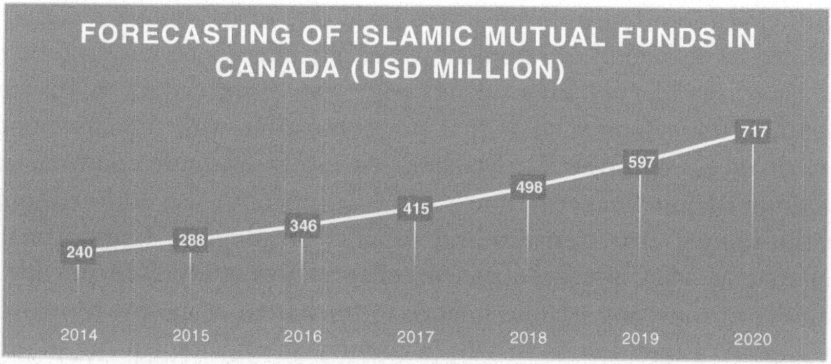

Fig. 8 Forecasting of Islamic mutual funds in Canada

Islamic mortgage is expected to be worth C$86 billion and C$110 billion by 2020 (Figs. 7 , 8).

9 Islamic Mutual Funds

Though there is domestic demand, the main opportunity for Islamic asset management is global. According to Thomson Reuters Lipper and fund reports, the total Islamic fund asset under management in Canada was US$240 million by the end of 2014.[15] Due to the rising interest of not only Muslim population but also non-Muslim population which is already inclined toward SRI, we expect the Islamic funds to grow by 20% p.a. The forecasted figures show that Islamic mutual funds can reach up to USD717 million by 2020.

10 Conclusion

As per Reinhart and Rogoff (2009), the long list of crises whether exchange rate or banking are actually debt crises. With the recent subprime crisis, the uncertainty with regard to sustainability of current financial system has also aggravated. As mentioned above, the quest for an alternative viable system has intensified. Islamic financial system being more resilient and less volatile due to its unique features is believed to be a good replacement, especially after its better response to the crisis. Broadly speaking, in this paper, we dispel certain myths surrounding the system such as it is not compatible with the contemporary finance, exclusively for Muslims. As more and more countries are adopting Islamic finance in one way or the other, we also outlined some of the unique characteristics and benefits of adopting Islamic financial system. More precisely, the objective of this study is to provide a viability of initiating Islamic finance in uncharted economy. Moreover, we explore a question as to why a country should implement Islamic finance. To achieve the objective, we have taken Canada as a case study. Based on the demography, established ethical market and existence of Islamic indices, and the mutual funds and its high rank in the Islamicity index, we argue that Canada could be one of the avenues to initiate Islamic financial system. We have also highlighted some of the economic benefits of such system in terms of its impact on economic growth. Additionally, we have also elaborated on how its risk-sharing characteristic and attachment to real economy could be beneficial for Canadian economy in terms of lowering the risk of banking crises and stock market crashes. Moreover, we have also made certain forecast related to the growth of Islamic finance (Islamic home financing and Islamic mutual funds) based on the growth of mortgage financing and the trend in SRI. We have also estimated the growth of Sukuk market, if the government plans to finance a portion of their infrastructure projects through Sukuk issuance.

The successful implementation of Islamic finance requires massive human capital, and in that sense, Canada can learn from Malaysian experience. To start off, Canada can collaborate with universities like INCEIF for industrial trainings. Canada can also leverage upon the Islamic studies department of universities like British Columbia to offer Islamic finance and carry out academic research. Moreover, the government has to overcome some of the regulatory challenges that are mentioned above. More importantly, the issues related to tax implications have to be reviewed in order to provide Islamic financing a level playing ground.

As this study provides critical insights and answers to several questions with regard to the viability and the operability of implementing Islamic finance, it can also be useful for the other developed countries aiming to adopt Islamic financial system in near future.

Notes

1. See Islamic Financial Services Industry Stability Report, IFSB (2015) (Islamic Financial Services Board 2015).
2. http://www.bbc.co.uk/religion/0/23448808.
3. The statistics used in this section are obtained from reports published by Islamic Financial Services Board, Kuala Lumpur, Kuwait Finance House Research, Kuala Lumpur and Dubai Center for Islamic Banking and Finance, Dubai. The details can be found in References Sect.
4. We are indebted to H. Askari et al. (2012) for this discussion on risk sharing approach and its various other aspects.
5. World Islamic Banking Competitiveness Report (2016).
6. World Bank Treasury: How socially responsible investing can help bridge the gap between Islamic and conventional financial market.
7. Ibid.
8. Statistics Canada. "Immigration and Ethnocultural Diversity in Canada," (Accessed July 28, 2015) http://www12.statcan.gc.ca/nhs-enm/2011/assa/99-010-x/99-010-x2011001-eng.cfm.

9. Félio, Guy. 2012. Canadian Infrastructure Report Card. The Canadian Infrastructure Report Card: Ottawa, Canada. www.canadainfrastructure.ca.
10. http://www.statcan.gc.ca/tables-tableaux/sum-som/l01/cst01/famil53a-eng.htm.
11. http://www12.statcan.gc.ca/nhs-enm/2011/as-sa/99-010-x/99-010-x2011001-eng.cfm#a6.
12. http://www.crea.ca/housing-market-stats/national-average-price-map/.
13. http://www.globalpropertyguide.com/North-America/Canada/Price-History.
14. Staff writer. "Calling the faithful," The Economist, December 7, 2006. http://www.economist.com/node/8382406.
15. http://financial.thomsonreuters.com/en/products/data-analytics/financial-research/lipper-fund-research.html.

References

Al-Fawwaz, T. M., Alawneh, A. M., & Shawaqfeh, G. N. (2015). The impact of islamic finance on some macro economic variables (A case study of Jordan Islamic Bank). *Interdisciplinary Journal of Contemporary Research in Business, 7*(1), 236, 278.

Askari, H. (2012). Islamic finance, risk-sharing, and international financial stability. *Yale Journal of International Affairs, 7,* 1.

Askari, H., Iqbal, Z., Krichenne, N., & Mirakhor, A. (2010). *Stability of Islamic finance: Creating a resilient financial environment for a secure future.* Singapore: Wiley.

Askari, H., Iqbal, Z., Krichene, N., & Mirakhor, A. (2012). *Risk sharing in finance: The Islamic finance alternative.* Hoboken, NJ: Wiley.

Chapra, M. U. (2007). Challenges facing the islamic financial industry. In M. K. Hassan & M. K. Lewis (Eds.), *Handbook of Islamic banking* (pp. 325–360). Cheltenham: Edward Elgar.

Čihák, M., & Hesse, H. (2008). *Islamic banks and financial stability: An empirical analysis* (Working Papers, 1–29). International Monetary Fund.

Ernst and Young. (2016). *World Islamic banking competitiveness report: New realities new opportunities.* London: EY.

Gheeraert, L., & Weill, L. (2015). Does Islamic banking development favor macroeconomic efficiency? Evidence on the Islamic finance-growth nexus. *Economic Modelling, 47,* 32–39.

Imam, P. A., & Kpodar, K. (2015). Is Islamic banking good for growth? (Working Paper WP/15/81). Washington, DC: International Monetary Fund.

Islamic Financial Services Board. (2015). *Islamic financial services industry stability report.* IFSB: Kuala Lumpur.

Mirakhor, A. (2010). *Whither Islamic finance? Risk sharing in an age of crises* (No. 56341). Germany: University Library of Munich.

Mirakhor, A. (2012). *Islamic finance, risk sharing and macroeconomic policies* (No. 56338). Germany: University Library Of Munich.

Reinhart, C. M., & Rogoff. K. S. (2009). *This Time Is Different: Eight Centuries of Financial Folly.* Princeton, USA: Princeton University Press.

Stiglitz, J. (2003). Dealing with debt. *Harvard International Review, 25*(1), 54–60.

Islamic Finance, in the Age of Black Swans and Complexities, for a Multipolar World

Mughees Shaukat and Abbas Mirakhor

Abstract The recent financial developments have given rise to a developing consensus that the unipolar economic growth regime dominated by USA, Japan, and few European centers is under great stress. The consensus takes into consideration the present financial complexities, stresses, and strains, and the ensuing uncertainty surrounding the sustainability of the unipolar regime, which has given way to a shift toward a multipolar economic setup. Scholarship has already hinted on not only better trade and investment opportunities, but also on a much more resilient global economic growth that such a shift can bring. However, there are some major obstacles that need to be overcome in order to reap fully the desired benefits of multipolarity. Continuation of debt-based financing regime (the hallmarks of which are risk transfer

---

M. Shaukat (✉)
College of Banking and Financial Studies, Muscat, Oman
e-mail: mughees@cbfs.edu.om

A. Mirakhor
INCEIF the Global University of Islamic Finance, Kuala Lumpur, Malaysia
e-mail: abbasmirakhor@inceif.org

S.A.R. Rizvi and I. Saba (eds.), *Developments in Islamic Finance*, Palgrave CIBFR Studies in Islamic Finance, DOI 10.1007/978-3-319-59342-5_7

and risk shifting) will not necessarily allow the benefits of emerging multipolarity to accrue to the world economy. The new system can be more effective with a new regime of financing. Indications are that almost all emerging countries in Asia are actively considering risk sharing via Islamic finance as a possible alternative.

Keywords Multipolar regime · Debt stress · Complexity · Black swans · Risk sharing · Islamic finance

1 Introduction

By 2025, Brazil, India, Indonesia, Korea, and Russia are expected to join China as new growth poles in the global economy, according to a recent World Bank Global Development Horizon report (2011). The size, dynamism, and dominance in the forward and backward linkages in trade and investment of an economy are the criteria for selection. However, the central rationale for this fast-developing consensus is supported by the fact that the present unipolar regime, dominated by USA, is under ever-increasing debt stress, creating serious doubts about its sustainability. This has led to developments where (i) the balance of global growth is shifting from developed to emerging market economies leading to the emergence of a new global economic order; (ii) there will be a shift in the drivers and sources of global trade and investment flows; and (iii) the international reserve currency structure will move from a unitary to multicurrency regime. The evidence for the premise includes the fact that: (i) the emerging markets are leading the global growth; (ii) these economies have been a major source of origination of cross-border mergers and acquisition with a significant increase from US$27 billion in 1997 to US$254 billion in 2011 and from 576 deals to 2447 over the same period; (iii) emerging market economy corporates have increased the strength of their presence in the global financial markets as their borrowing increased from US$123 billion in 2000 to US$461 billion by the end of 2010; and (iv) their borrowing costs have reduced. It is for the first time that the emerging markets have gained the status from being plain borrowers to becoming plain creditors (Sheng 2009).

There are indications that the shift in the global economic growth drivers which began in the 1990s has accelerated. During the period of 2000–2008, twenty-nine countries had achieved sustained growth rates of 7% or higher for 25 years or more, thus cushioning global growth performance. Eleven of the 29 countries were from Africa. Among these, the Asian economies were the best performers. The United Nations Economic and Social Commission for Asia and Pacific 2011 considers the region as the most dynamic in the global economy, growing at 8.8% in 2010 and forecasted to grow at 7.3% in 2011. This compares well with the anemic growth performance of the countries at the center of the present unipolar system. One of the most important implications of the shift is the potential for the emergence of multiple international reserve currencies. The Global Development Horizon, 2011, suggests three possible scenarios for the future: (i) continued dominance of the US$ as the international reserve currency; (ii) possibility of the SDR as the international reserve currency; and (iii) emergence of at least three international reserve currencies. In the first scenario, evidence suggests that the US$ is being used less and less as an official reserve in invoicing of international transactions, as an anchor for other exchange rates, and in denominating international claims. The SDR, while originally designed with the intention of serving as the international reserve currency, has never been allowed to serve that function, and it is not likely now. What is more likely, according to the report, is that Chinese currency will emerge as the third international reserve currency alongside the US$ and the euro. China is now the largest exporter in the world. As Chinese corporates and banks increase their activities across the world, they are likely to settle their trade, track accounts, and book their profits in renminbi. Chinese sovereign wealth funds are now among the largest in the world, China has large international reserves, and debt and equities are being issued in renminbi. Consequently, expectation of its emergence as an international reserve currency is well founded. However, there are few major obstacles which if not confronted may not only threaten the emergence of a multipolar regime, but also could lead to a failure in reaping the full benefits from such a development.

2 Obstacles to the Emergence of Multiple Growth Poles

The emergence of multiple growth poles in the global economy has potential benefits, the most important of which is greater resilience of *emerging market economies and developing countries* to idiosyncratic shocks similar to what triggered the 2007/2008 crisis. Additionally, greater trade and investment opportunities between the emerging markets of the South and low-income developing countries can be enormously helpful and effective in accelerating growth, development, and poverty reduction in the latter. China has been doing that effectively since the early 1990s particularly in the low-income countries of Africa. There are, however, major obstacles to overcome. These include, inter alia, the architecture and governance of global finance. The former is woefully inadequate in providing requisite infrastructure of supervision and regulation to accommodate balanced growth of global finance. The fact is that years after the beginning of the global crisis, *there is no global agreement on cross-border financial flows, there is no internationally agreed sovereign—debt workout mechanism,* and there is no effective representative global structure for policy coordination. Moreover, the existing structures are non-representative and suffer from high democratic deficit. They make policies and impose standards and codes of conduct and international best practices on the rest of the world without an effective representation of much of the world's most dynamically growing economies.

Last but not least, one of the obstacles to the global economic recovery and emergence of multiple growth poles is the important structure of global finance, which is overwhelmingly dominated by debt-creating flows. As the latest financial crisis suggested, this structure is imposing anew a great deal of burden and stress on the recovery and growth of the global economy. Perhaps, the stresses and shocking financial events of recent months in Europe as well as its breakdown in the USA are signs of regime uncertainty. The regime of interest rate-based finance is the source of much of the economic and financial uncertainty tightly gripping the global system. Moreover, the continuing adverse economic and social consequences, as well as the failure of significant policy actions to elicit the desired response, seem to provide evidence that the global financial system displays the characteristics of a "*complex system.*" Added to the shock of occurrence of "fat tail" events, increased poverty and worsening distribution of income and wealth in individual and collective economies have intensified regime uncertainty.

2.1 Complexity of the Interest Rate-Based Debt Finance

Discussions on the complexity of the present system and its connections with the forces which render the system uncertain and unstable seem to have surged. Complex systems are dynamical and are characterized by nonlinearity (Lorenz 1993). These systems are governed by feedback loop mechanisms *where small, marginal changes in the system have a significantly large impact on the overall behavior.* Such arrangements are all characterized by "bifurcation points" at which system can move either to more stability and order or to chaos (Progogine 1997). There has to be zero defect policy for the system to work in an ordered way. Unavoidably, complex systems are uncontrollable and innately carry with them large elements of uncertainty and ambiguity (Wheatley 1992).

It appears that the complexity of the system is playing an added role in intensifying the system's fragility. Thus, the nexus becomes a worthy exploration. However, it would help to first note what is meant by a system and indicate differences between simple, complicated, and complex systems. A system is defined as "*set of elements standing in interrelations*" to one another (von Bertalanffy 1969: 38). Or, as Meadows (2000: 2) elaborates: "*A system is a set of things—people, cells, molecules, or whatever—interconnected in such a way that they produce their own pattern of behaviour over time.*" How predictable that "own pattern of behaviour over time" may be depends on the nature of the system in terms of the degree of simplicity or complexity of the rules governing the interrelationship among its elements. A simple system is quite predictable because of the simplicity of its operational rules. For example, old cars had simple starting operations: placing keys in the ignition to start the engine. This represents a simple and predictable system. Complicated systems contain subsets of simple systems. Their complicated nature is often related not only to the scale but also to issues of coordination of specialized expertise. In contrast to the old cars, newer and more technically advanced automobiles represent complicated systems. Instead of a key in the ignition, push button remotes are used to start an engine. Despite considerably more complicated technologies, modern automobiles still represent predictable systems.

Complex systems contain both complicated and simple subsidiary parts, but are not reducible to either (Goodwin 1994) since they too have special requirements, including an understanding of unique local conditions. *Such systems are dynamical and are characterized by nonlinearity.* Interdependency and interconnectedness of all the heterogeneous elements that build up such a system, where each part is doing its own thing, carry the ability to create emergent phenomenon (crowding effect) with scaling, criticality, and self-organization capacity, all in the absence of any central controller or coordinator (Johnson 2007). These systems are operated, ruled, and governed by *feedback loops.* Such arrangements are all characterized by "bifurcation points" at which system can move either to more stability and order or to chaos (Progogine 1997). *There has to be zero defect policy for the system to work in an ordered way. In such a system, a small marginal change is capable of creating large impact on the global behavior of the system with the added attribute of nonlinearity (Lorenz* 1993*). Unavoidably, complex systems are uncontrollable and innately carry with them large elements of uncertainty and ambiguity (Wheatley* 1992*).* Over the last several decades, the view that economic reality is somehow fundamentally complex has increasingly taken hold among economists, not only those focused on abstract theory but also even policymakers as well.

There are nonlinearities: This can be clearly observed from an increasingly volatile nature of the financial markets and frequent booms and busts. The market is not governed by assumptions of normal distribution and Brownian motion. Instead, it is irregular and nonlinear (Mandelbrot and Hudson 2004). Extreme events, involving collective phenomena (resulting from the iteration of nonlinear interactions), such as herding or alignment (as seems to occur in bubbles and crashes), are an integral part of scaling theory (itself a feature of complexity). Speculative bubbles then correspond to scaling, criticality, and a self-organization process. Econophysicists argue that stock market crashes and other economic phenomena (that are often puzzling from the perspective of standard economic theory, "outliers" in fact) are an entirely natural consequence of the view that economic systems, such as financial markets, are complex. Hence, extreme behavior (nonlinearity) and self-organization in a system are a strong indication that complexity is involved. Progogine (1980, 1989, and 1997) who used the notion of "point of bifurcation" suggests that there comes a point at which the system can proceed to more order or to disorder. Interconnectedness: (i) on a macro level, each financial subsystem is interlinked to create the whole financial sector which itself is a subsystem of the whole economic order. (ii) The web of counterparties and common exposures, containing multiple agents of different types (producers and consumers; risk averse and risk takers; firms and individuals; etc.), and interacting in such a way as to generate the "emergent properties" and dynamics of economic systems and subsystems—in the absence of any central controller (Johnson 2007). However, what necessarily sets the dynamics of these interactions and the emergent properties toward disorder and chaos is a third interconnection termed as the "*complex debt structure*" (Askari et al. 2012).

Many have conceded to the complexity and the resulting nonlinearity of the financial system. While talking about the complexity and nonlinearity dynamics of the financial system, where small shocks anywhere in the system are having contagious effects on the global behavior of the system, Paulos (2003: 172–174) suggests as follows:

> Certainly, economists and financial experts appear to take too little notice of the complicated connections among the economic variables, even the more clearly defined ones. Interest rates, for example, have an impact on unemployment rates, which in turn influence revenues; budget deficits affect trade deficits, which sway interest rates and exchange rates; corporate fraud influences consumer confidence, which may depress the stock market and alter other indices; natural business cycles of various periods are superimposed on one another; an increase in some quantity or index positively (or negatively) feeds back on another, reinforcing or weakening it and being reinforced or weakened in turn. Few of these associations are accurately described by a straight-line graph or linearity assumptions. Nonlinear dynamics —more popularly known as chaos theory—doesn't deal with anarchist treatises or surrealist manifestoes but with the behaviour of so-called nonlinear systems. The systems that depict non-linearity may be thought of as any collection of parts whose interactions and connections are described by nonlinear rules or equations. That is to say, the equations' variables may be multiplied together, raised to powers, and so on. As a consequence the system's parts are not necessarily linked in a proportional manner as they are, for example, in a bathroom scale or a thermometer; doubling the magnitude of one part will not double that of another—nor will outputs be proportional to inputs. Not surprisingly, trying to predict the precise long-term behaviour of such systems is often futile… this non-predictability is the result not of randomness, but of *complexity* too great to fathom.

In the early 1940s, a British mathematician, Alan Turing, was perhaps the first modern scientist to formulate complexity. The hallmark of his contribution was a paper he wrote about the growth of biological system in which he put forward the idea of "morphogenesis" (Turing 1952). He showed that a biological system described by two simple equations with feedback loops among the variables was capable of behaving in totally unpredictable, complex patterned behavior. A decade later, an American meteorologist, Edward N. Lorenz, tried to predict the weather with computers, but instead gave rise to the modern field of chaos theory and developed models with feedback loops to increase the accuracy of weather forecast (Lorenz 1963). In another paper (Lorenz 1993), he showed how a small twiddling of parameters in a model could produce vastly different behavior, transforming regular, periodic events into a seemingly random chaotic pattern. In summary, his models showed two things: unpredictability of weather systems and the significantly large impact of small, marginal changes in local individual element's behavior on the global behavior of the system. This last point made famous "*The Butterfly Effect*" also known as "*sensitive dependence on initial conditions*".[1] However, Benoit Mandelbrot while reaching the same conclusion using a relatively simple equation with feedback interaction claimed further that all the theories in finance were wrong because they relied on Gaussian (normal) probability distributions and the Brownian motion, both of which assume regularities. He pointed out that nearly all economic and financial variables, particularly stock prices and commodity prices, behaved irregularly.[2] Their behavior, Mandelbrot argued, was better described by "Fractal Geometry and mathematics" than by Gaussian distribution and Brownian motion (Mandelbrot and Hudson 2004) as they are instead characterized, Mandelbrot suggested, by jumps rather than smooth motion. Since finance theories were wrong, so would be their predictions; the recent financial crisis has vindicated his claims.

Peters (1996) argued the need for a new way of looking at markets behavior. He claimed (similar to Mandelbrot) that the assumptions of efficient markets and rational investors in mainstream theories are a fallacy. On the basis of "chaos theory," he showed that in fact markets are nonlinear dynamic systems with feedback effects, criticality levels, as well as fractal in nature. He further argued that such a system is always far from equilibrium. Chorafas (1994) echoes both Mandelbrot and Peters and suggests that neither linearity nor the hypotheses of normal distribution can provide the right support in understanding markets. Financial analysts have to turn their attention to non-traditional means of research and analysis in figuring out financial market behavior. These new tools, he argues, come under the heading of "Complexity Theory" and include tools such as "non-linearities, bifurcations, chaos theory, fractals and other fuzzy engineering techniques."

Johnson (2007) while conferring the complexity of the financial markets suggests that complex systems have a tendency to move from order to disorder and vice versa. While arguing that such movements cannot be predicted, *for financial markets, crises are actually a move toward an ordered state, sufficing that the ordered state of such a complex system is actually a disorder.* Similarly, Zambelli and George (2012: 4) in their latest book titled: *Nonlinearity, Complexity and Randomness in Economics*, argues as follows:

> Those of us who have marvelled at the non-linear feedback loops between asset prices in illiquid markets and the funding illiquidity of financial institutions exposed to these asset prices through mark-to-market accounting, margin requirements, calls for additional collateral, etc. will appreciate what is lost by this castration of the macroeconomic models. Threshold effects, critical mass, tipping points, non-linear accelerators – they are all out of the window. Those of us who worry about endogenous uncertainty arising from the interactions of boundedly rational market participants cannot but scratch our heads at the insistence of the mainline models that all uncertainty is exogenous and additive. The first lesson to draw from the current crisis within Economics is clearly that our models must embrace non-linearity: linearized models with their saddle point dynamics and 'jump variables' no longer serve any useful purpose.

Schwarcz (2009) argue that the current economic crisis illustrates a critical need for new and fundamental understanding of the structure and dynamics of economic networks. Economic systems are increasingly built on interdependencies of both behavior and information, leading to a global economy where credit and investment, trade and input–output flows, and research and innovation all occur at a truly world scale that gives rise to a hugely complex system that is difficult to predict and control. Moreover, some interdependencies become obvious only during and after the crisis—*such as tight global credit couplings*—developing as self-fulfilling phenomena, without precursory signatures.

> The complexity of the modern global economy is exacerbated among others, by the speed and scope of credit spread across national and globally networked markets, with variable intensity of ties and of scale. A small shock in the debt repayment- through either endogenous or exogenous means—can lead to mass scale effects; making the attempts to understand

> or control the emergent and volatile networks very difficult indeed. In particular, the danger of cascading failures or the spread of opportunistic behaviour through the economic networks is greater today than ever. Self-feeding effects, reinforcing each other through a co-evolving network, can lead to large-scale and abrupt consequences that may be hard to anticipate and tackle

Ilya Progogine (1980, 1989, 1997) suggested that for a complex system, there is a "point of bifurcation", a moment of truth, for the system to choose which path it follows. Chaos theory suggests that a complex system approaching a bifurcation point becomes so sensitive that it can amplify small changes into large feedbacks. Decisions made at such a point lead the system either toward greater chaos or toward higher order (Mirakhor and Hamid 2009: 231). It appears that the "point of bifurcation" has been operating to increase regime uncertainty. At every "bifurcation point" reached, policymakers seem to have made decisions that have rendered the system highly risky and more unstable, heightening the system's sensitivity to register events that can be termed as the "black swan" events. Hence, there is increasing uncertainty regarding the stability and sustainability of the interest rate-based debt financing regime.

2.2 Unipolar Regime, Debt Stress, and the Black Swans

A serious problem facing the global economy today is the situation of debt overhang which has made the present system to reach a point of criticality and bifurcation, creating debilitating fears of contagion and recurrence of full-fledged global crisis. Krugman (1996) coined the term "debt overhang" and asserted it as a situation in which "*A country has a debt over-hang problem when the expected present value of potential future resource transfers in less than the debt*". The fall of the Soviet Union consolidated the power of the dollar-based unipolar international trade and financial system until the 2007/2008 global crisis. The stress and strain in the unipolar system and its associated arrangement were becoming apparent in the 1990s as Japan followed by The Asian Tigers,

Russia, Argentina, and Brazil were sending distress signals. Neither the signals nor the lessons of these crises made any significant impact on the way the centers of the dollar-based unipolar system were conducting policies. The regime was quick to impose policy and structural reforms, standards, and codes through the international financial institutions (IFIs) in which the USA–Western Europe–Japan held major sway. However, the center of the system itself was slow to adopt the prescriptions it was writing for the emerging market economies and developing countries. The case in point was the diagnostic device: financial sector assessment as well as other best international practices and codes which the IMF required from all its members. The USA was one of the last to adopt them, but much too late to prevent the idiosyncratic trigger of the global crisis.

Consequently, The Global Risks Report 2014 analyzed 50 global risks in terms of impact, likelihood, and interconnections, based on a survey of over 1000 experts from industry, government, and academia. The report highlights wealth gaps—severe income disparity—followed by unsustainable government debt—chronic fiscal imbalances—as the top two most prevalent global risks. IMF (2013) suggests that failure to deal with old and new risks risked propelling the 5-year-old crisis into a fresh chronic phase.

It can be asserted that when risks become high, so does the lack of ability to understand, control, and mitigate the risks. This is a situation where risks get transformed into their stronger cases of "uncertainty" and "ambiguity." Frank Knight explained that, at times, decisions are made based on available probability distribution of expected events. This is decision making under risk. Unlike risk, however, uncertainty describes a situation where a known probability distribution is not available, but it is still possible to make decisions with some subjective estimates of probability of outcomes of actions or decisions. In the 1960s, this view was modified to cover circumstances under which human cognitive ability and information availability are so constrained that even subjective assessment of outcomes was not possible. Ambiguity arises under such circumstances where the intensity of "ignorance" can create paralysis in the decision making (Erbas and Mirakhor 2007).

The result is an ideal recipe for the occurrence of those events which were deemed as highly improbable or never occurring. As a result, an important concept has been added to the economic vernacular, termed as "Black Swan" events. Taleb (2010 [2007]) the inventor of the term refers to them as those events which (i) usually lie outside the realm of regular expectations, because nothing in the past can convincingly point to its possibility. As a result, the probability of the occurrence of such events is extremely low, (ii) even though they have a low probability of occurrence; however, when they do occur, the events carry an extreme impact; (iii) lastly, in spite of its outlier status, human nature makes us concoct explanations for its occurrence after the fact, making it explainable and predictable.

Recently, the global system has experienced events that would have been thought of as low-probability events not long ago. These include, inter alia, the downgrading of USA from its "AAA" rating, the collapse of the much hailed Eurozone, the effort by Switzerland to convince the world that Swiss franc is not a safe haven, the Brazilian suggestion of bailout of advanced economy by emerging markets, China's contemplation of buying Italy's debt, and the Libor rate fixing. Cyprus's provocation of removing deposit guarantees on certain amounts of deposits. The list can go on. However, looming in the background of the present uncertainties in the global economy, there is a potential event termed as "*the mother of all black swans*" the effects of which may be chaotic to the global economy: contagion-riddled events of *sovereign default.*

It can be observed that the increasing complexity and the ensuing occurrence of black swans and nonlinearity of the debt dynamics is a pure demonstration of the Quranic concept of "YAMHAQ". Allah swt tells us about the debt dynamics in verse 276 of chapter 2 of the Quran: "***Yamhaq****hu Allah o arRibawaYurbiasSadaqat*" (Allah swt annuls, obliterates arRiba and increases Sadaqat). The part that is most relevant here is the first part of the verse "***Yamhaq***hu Allah o arRiba". Reference, for example, to Al-Mu'jam Al-Waseet, Maqayees al-Lughah, and Mufradaat al-Quran reveals that "Yamhaq" that makes the "Mahq" of riba means to decrease, to destroy completely, to take away the blessings from a thing, to negate or cancel out the positive impact of a thing, or to erase suddenly. It is thus a state of sudden and rapid decline, with the speed of destruction picking up acceleration (Shaukat 2014).

In order to give evidence of the adverse and nonlinear debt dynamics, that is to signify the Quranic "*Mahq*" in full operation in the global economy, the findings of Reinhart and Rogoff (2010, 2011) and Kaminsky and Reinhart (1999) put forward among the most finely textured, historical, analysis of the financial crisis.[3] The data covers seventy countries in across all regions. The range of variables encompasses external and domestic debt, trade, GNP, inflation, exchange rates, interest rates, and commodity prices. The coverage spans eight centuries, going back to the date of independence or well into the colonial period for some countries. The authors showed that crises whatever label they carried—exchange rate crisis or banking crisis—have been at root debt crises (Reinhart and Rogoff 2010).

The authors refers to the nonlinearity of such consequences as the "*Deadly Ds*": Sharp economic "*downturns*" follow banking crises; with government revenues dragged down, fiscal "*deficits*" worsen; deficits lead to more "*debt*"; as debt piles up, rating "*downgrades*"[4] follow and "*defaults*" ensue, the result of a vicious "*debt circle*" (see also Mauldin and Tepper 2011). The studies revealed that 3 years after a financial crisis, central government debt increases, on average, by about *86 percent*, implying that the fiscal burden of banking crisis extends far beyond the common cost of the bailouts. Moreover, real housing price declines on average *35 percent*, stretching out over 6 years. Equity price collapses on average *56 percent* with the downturn spanning around *4 years*.

Similarly profound are the unemployment rates which rise at an average of *7 percent*, lasting over 4 years. In some cases, these unemployment levels reach as high as in the range of *20 percent* to over *50 percent* including youth unemployment. Such scenarios are presently pervasive in a number of European centers, for example, the case of PIIGS nations[5] (Table 1). Real GDP per capita falls (from peak to trough) on an average of over *9 percent* or more, the duration of the downturn averages at least 2–3 years, and production levels decline exponentially.

In another study, Reinhart et al. (2012) demonstrate the large adverse impact of debt overhang on economic growth. A study of 26 episodes of past overhangs revealed that: (i) the duration of an average overhang

Table 1 Unemployment stats

Country	Youth unemployment (Jan 2012) (%)	Overall unemployment (Jan 2012)
Greece	55	26
Spain	50	26.5
Italy	32	9
Portugal	35	15
Ireland	32	15

Source Author's own

episode is 23 years; (ii) during the overhang period, growth declines by 1% over the period; and (iii) the loss of growth and the long duration of the overhang imply "*that cumulative shortfall in output from debt overhang is potentially massive*[6]" (see also, Shaukat 2014). Similarly, Arcand et al. (2012) while using different empirical approaches also showed that there can indeed be "too much" finance. In particular, similar to Reinhart and Rogoff (2011), their results suggested that finance starts having a negative effect on output growth when credit to the private sector reaches on average 60–100% of GDP. However, Reinhart et al. (2003) while introducing the concept of "debt intolerance"—which manifests itself in the extreme duress many economies experience at seemingly manageable debt—argue that "safe" external debt-to-GDP thresholds for debt-intolerant countries could be as low as 15%.

A central and overwhelming cause of the Asian crisis was debt in all its dimensions. The global financial crisis has been analyzed voluminously, and a variety of reasons have been given for the crisis. By far, the most comprehensive has been the study by Reinhart and Rogoff (2010), which conveys a central message that all financial crises, whether currency or banking crisis, are at root debt crises. IMF had already focused on this issue in its post-Asian crisis diagnostics and had recommended that emerging markets and developing countries must avoid debt-creating flows and rely on foreign direct investment. The safe level of government debt-to-GDP ratio was less than 25% according to these recommendations. Reinhart and Rogoff (2010) study, "Growth in a Time of Debt", confirmed that a government debt-to-GDP ratio beyond 30% begins to stress growth. They studied 44 countries for which data was available over a period of 200 years, dividing debt categories into under 30, 30–60, 60–90, and over 90%. They showed that growth comes under stress in all these categories, but becomes quite seriously impaired at higher levels, so that when the ratio reaches 100%, interest payments equal the nominal GDP.

The above can be further supported by the findings of Frank Ramsey who in 1920s analyzed the interaction of the rate of population growth, the growth of market-determined interest rate, and the growth of economy to deduce the following: If the rate of economic growth exceeded the other rates, i.e., the market-determined rate of interest and the rate of population growth, the economy would grow. A steady state was when all the three rates were in equilibrium; however, when the market-determined interest rate growth surpassed the growth of the economy and the growth of population, economic activity would begin a downward spiral. He found that whenever the interest rate growth surpassed the other two rates, economic progress was dampened (Ramsey 1928). In this context, it is worth noting that the artificially low interest rates contrived by central banks' easy monetary policy may have disrupted economies and financial markets and spread financial chaos as recent debt crises have clearly established. There seems to be an adverse debt dynamics at work in the global economy presently where, even at artificially low interest rates, the rates of growth of economies are not sufficient to validate the growing debt.[7]

While the emerging economies learned the lessons of 1997/1998 crises, put their macroeconomic policy house in order, reduced their exposure to sudden stops, and accumulated reserves, most advanced economies went in the opposite direction. They reduced their savings, increased consumption, ran fiscal deficits, and accumulated large debts. Empirical research suggests that debt-to-GDP ratio of the richest members of the G20 will reach 120% mark by 2014, while by 2020, the USA and the other major European centers would amass a ratio of at least 150%, with Japan and U.K going to 300 and 200%, respectively. Even more disconcerting is the projected interest rate paths on their debts which would increase from 5 to 10% in all cases, and as high as 27% in U.K (BIS 2010). These countries suffer from high unemployment, fiscal instability, low capacity utilization, and high debt and leverage. Accordingly, growth is unlikely to provide a source of debt relief. Rogoff (2011) suggests that there are now $200 trillion of financial paper in the global economy, nearly 75%, or US$150 trillion is in interest-bearing debt. The picture becomes more disconcerting when the ensuing disequilibrium is realized. While the global GDP is growing at 3%, the debt is increasing at 7%. It would take 24 years for the global GDP to double itself, while a mere 10 years for the global debt to get twice as large. *It is thus difficult to imagine how this massive debt volume can be validated by the underlying productive capacity of the global economy. It is "Yamhaqhu Allah o arRiba"*. It appears that the debt dynamics in global financial system has again made the system reach a point of criticality and bifurcation, where a sovereign default by one country can prove chaotic to the global economy. According to John Mauldin and Jonathan Tepper (2011):

> When things are unstable, it isn't the last grain of sand that causes the pile to collapse or the slight breeze that causes the ruler on your finger tip to fall. Those are proximate causes. They are the closet reasons at hand for the collapse. The real reason though, is the remote cause, the farthest reason. The farthest reason is the underlying instability of the system itself.

Thus far, the search for ways and means of reducing the instability of the interest-based debt system has focused only on improving regulatory/supervisory structure and few reforms of financial system. Much less effort has been devoted to finding an alternative paradigm. Askari et al. (2012: ix) suggest as follows:

> reforms are little more than a "bandaging" of the current financial system: higher levels of capital; breaking up of financial institutions; regulation to include all financial institutions; measures to limit risk taking and to increase transparency, and more. But it is difficult to see how any of these changes will eliminate the likelihood of future financial crises. Higher capital requirements would reduce bank lending, money creation and leveraging, but there is always a chance that bad loans could still wipe out a bank's capital. Similarly, limiting the size of financial institutions would reduce, but not eliminate, systemic risk and the need for bailouts.

> Increasing transparency in the packaging, pricing, and settling of derivatives would afford investors more information on pricing and reduce, but again not eliminate, systemic risk. And on and on.

The question arises as to whether there is such an alternative to the present dominant global finance system that could suit well the prospects of "Economic Multipolarity." *Perhaps a more practical alternative would be to step back from targeting the interest rate mechanism and focus on the incentive structure that has rendered the interest rate-based debt financing such a destabilizing force in the global system. This can be accomplished by reorienting the system from relying on risk transfer and risk shifting to risk sharing—the essence of Islamic finance.*

3 Risk-Sharing Finance Regime as an Alternative

Risk sharing—the essence of Islamic finance—has a number of desirable characteristics that endorse it as the ideal method of financing in the age of information superhighway. It weakens the rationale for existence of age-old debt financing, i.e., lack of information and all associated informational problems (Mirakhor 2011). Classical Arabic Lexicons of the Qur'an define contracts of exchange (*al-bay'*) as contracts involving exchange of property rights claims in which there are expectations of gains and probability of losses, see, for example, Al-Tahquiq Fi Kalamat Al-Quran Al-Karim, Lisan Al-Arab, Mufradat Alfaz Al Quran, Arabic Lexicon, among others. These sources define *al-bay'* as "*mubadalati al-maali bi al-maal.*" In English, this can be rendered as "*the exchange of one set of property rights claim for another*". By entering into contracts of exchange, parties improve their welfare by exchanging the risks of economic undertakings, thus allowing division of labor and specialization (see Mirakhor 2011). Since in the Verse the contract of exchange (al-bay) appears first and the prohibition of *riba* thereafter, it can be argued that requiring contracts to be based on exchange constitutes a necessary condition and "no-*riba*" the sufficient condition of existence of an Islamic financial system. Together, these conditions constitute the organizing principle of that system. The necessary condition (*al-bay'*) and sufficient condition (no-*riba*) must be met for a contract to be considered Islamic. "A careful consideration of all the permissible contract modes that have reached us reveals them to be basically risk sharing contracts. The instruments designed to financially empower them must also be risk sharing instruments".

Historically, the proposition asserted by Muslim scholars and layman has been that prohibition of riba contracts renders Islamic finance a potent alternative to conventional finance. This is valid only when Islamic finance operates on risk sharing basis rather than risk transfer, which is the hallmark of conventional finance whose operations have culminated in repeated and, at times, devastating crises. In brief, basic value propositions of risk-sharing finance are as follows: (i) close correspondence between the real sector of the economy and its financial sector, as a result of which the rate of return in the real sector determines the rate of return to the financial sector rather than the reverse; (ii) increased resilience and stability of the financial system and the economy; (iii) financial inclusion, poverty reduction, and shared economic growth and prosperity; (iv) expanded opportunities for entrepreneurship and innovation; and (iv) greater efficiency of resource allocation. These propositions have been argued in detail elsewhere and will not be elaborated here due to focus constraint. Those interested can refer to relevant published books and research papers on this topic.[8]

Research has demonstrated sizeable potential welfare benefits of risk sharing (see, for example, van Wincoop 1999; Kim et al. 2005; Lee and Shin 2008). Analyses of the pre-crises data show a fast-growing, debt-creating process in the global financial system with increasingly tenuous links with the growth of the real economy. Although equity portfolio and foreign direct investment flows were growing at a more rapid pace than debt-creating flows before the global crisis, their magnitudes were not significant enough to make a dent in the low level of risk-sharing coefficients in the empirical studies. For example, a study by Kim, S. et al. (2005) showed that even in the fast-growing East Asia—10 countries—the size of the coefficient of risk sharing was very small and some were negative (Indonesia and Malaysia). Increased debt-creating flows, a characteristic of financial globalization in the run-up of

2007/2008 crises, do not improve risk sharing, as they either transfer or shift risk. More importantly, risk shifting or risk transfer financial transactions lead global finance toward decoupling from real sector activities with the growth of the former outpacing that of the latter by double-digit multiples, intensifying the risk of "sudden stops" [Mirakhor et al. (2012)]. Even the emergence of a multipolar global economy may not improve risk sharing across the globe. Perhaps, the most important reason for this state of affairs is the reliance of global finance on debt-creating flows.

Islam is a rules-based system in which a network of prescribed rules governs the socioeconomic–political life of the society. Compliance with these rules renders the society a union of mutual support by requiring humans to share the risks of life (Mirakhor 2011a, b).The epistemological roots of risk sharing as an organizing principle of Islamic financial system are discernible from the verse 275 of chapter 2 of the Quran. This verse, in part, decrees that all economic and financial transactions are conducted via contracts of exchange (al-Bay') and not through interest-based debt contracts (al-Riba). Since in the verse the contract of exchange appears first and no-riba thereafter, it can be argued that requiring contracts to be based on exchange constitutes a necessary condition and "no-riba" the sufficient condition of existence of an Islamic financial system. Together, these conditions constitute the organizing principle of that system. The necessary condition (al-Bay') and sufficient condition (no-riba) must be met for a contract to be considered Islamic (Mirakhor 2011a, b).

The method of finance that renders payoffs to financial assets contingent on the outcome of economic activities—rather than on ex ante fixed rates that must be paid as contractual obligation of the debtor regardless of the outcome of the project for which it was borrowed—is technically known as state-contingent financing. Arrow-Debreu (1971), proof of existence of a stable equilibrium for a competitive economy, required that all assets must be state contingent, i.e., their payoffs depended on the outcome of economic activities. Residual payments to equity shares of modern corporations are the best examples of state-contingent claims. One justification for rapid globalization was that it would increase interaction in the human community and create a "global village". Risk sharing will do just that since it would require a familiarity among partners to a risk-sharing contract to make it work. As demonstrated by the recent crisis, dealing at "arms-length", a much-heralded characteristic of debt financing has made shifting risks from financiers to taxpayers, without their knowledge or consent, a much easier task. Because of its contingent character, a risk sharing contract requires close coordination between maturities, values, and payoffs of assets and liabilities sides of the balance sheet. These would move simultaneously in the same direction in response to changes in asset prices. In an economy dominated by state-contingent, risk sharing finance, there would have to be a close correspondence between the real sector activities and the financial sector, as the rates of return to the former would determine the rate of return to the latter. This alone would impose a limitation on credit expansion and leverage since these would increase only to accommodate growth in the real sector. These and other characteristics assure the stability of the financial sector [Askari et al. (2010)].

4 Risk Sharing as "Value Preposition" of Islamic Finance

It can be argued that the notion of risk-sharing financing could be framed as the "value proposition" of Islamic finance. Envisioned as real sector driven, the system is predominantly equity based where real savings are placed in the real sector, for example, in private or public projects. A pivotal feature of the dynamics is that the Islamic financial system is protected from unbacked credit expansion since banks do not contract interest-bearing loans and do not create and destroy money.[9] It is thus assumed that in an Islamic bank, there will be a maturity match between deposits and investment (with no need for asset and liability management). Short-term deposits may finance short-term trade operations, with bank purchasing merchandise or raw materials and selling to other companies; liquidity is replenished as proceeds from sales operation are generated. For longer-term investment, longer-term funds are used. There is hence greater interdependence and close relationship between investment and deposit yields, since banks primarily accept investments on the basis of profit–loss sharing. The funds to the enterprise are also provided on the same basis.

The dynamics would also in turn translate into a coordinated asset/liability maturity structure, as well as value matching. In addition to the prospect of instantaneous equilibrium between the asset and liability sides of the financial/banking system, there would also be asset/liability risk matching. While the individual financial institutions engaged in investment activities face the given risks, in and of themselves, these are not systemic and do not impact the overall stability of the financial system, as this system is immune to speculative mania, liquidity expansion, and instability of returns. The latter is assured via the same coordinated asset/liability value or maturity structure of the institutions. If asset prices decline, so will the liabilities, unlike what happens in a system dominated by interest-based debt contracts.[10]

Apart from providing the above ingredients of financial resilience and stability, the risk-sharing-based Islamic finance would also serve better the objectives of financial inclusion, poverty reduction, and shared economic prosperity via efficient resource allocation. The objective of efficient resource allocation is central to growth and stability of any financial system, allowing financial resources to receive their true opportunity cost. In an interest-based debt system, the financial resources appear not to be receiving their opportunity cost. This has led to misallocation of financial resources through "financial repression," a term coined in the 1970s. Risk sharing (Islamic finance) corrects this inefficiency.

Repression occurs when the prices of resources do not reflect their opportunity cost. It was thought, in the 1970s, that developing countries suffer from financial repression since interest rate was administered by the governments and directed lending. Consequently, the price of financial resources did not reflect the true opportunity cost of financing. As a result, the mantra that developing countries needed to "get the prices right" became the cornerstone of financial liberalization movement later enshrined in the "Washington Consensus." Liberalization meant removing barriers on prices of all resources to achieve their opportunity cost, defined as the next best alternative use of a resource. Opportunity cost of financial resources was, however, an exception since its opportunity cost was not the next best use of funds in the productive sector of the economy, but the "market rate of interest." Hence, a distortion in the use of financial resources was created because of what James Tobin termed "deviation between market valuation of capital and its replacement cost." Tobin further argued that this deviation is policy induced since monetary policy had a significant impact on the "market rate of interest," meaning that, just as in developing countries, the "market rate of interest" in advanced economies was also "administered" leading to financial repression.

The phenomenon of financial repression created a wedge between return to equity reflecting the rate of return to productive activities and the rate of interest. Islamic finance avoids this inefficiency given the rate of return to finance would be the real sector driven where financial resources are ultimately deployed. Immediately, the system renders a tight coupling between the financial and the real sectors, and the financial sector is found fulfilling its real aim, i.e., *serving the real sector*. It will hence be the returns to the real sector driving the economic outcomes. In this sense, Islamic finance is true financial liberalization. Data reveals that, globally, the average rate of return to the real sector is about 15–20%, a sizable multiple of the rate of interest ranging from negative to zero to 5–7%.

Given the importance of credit in the current financial and economic model, if credit supply is constrained by increasing its price, i.e., increasing interest rates, then a reverse of the above dynamics is achieved. High interest rates lower investments, which in turn lower consumption leading to a buildup in inventories and lowering growth in national output. Fallout is an increase in unemployment. If the decline in employment is more pronounced, consumption and investment decline further which further affects the national output. In case this decline continues for more than two consecutive quarters, then an economic recession is upon us. The dynamics help recall Keynes's criticism of capitalism. In his article published in Economic Journal Symposium in 1932, Keynes explicitly associated two "evils" to capitalism. First is capitalism's inability to create full employment and second is its ability to create highly skewed income and wealth distributions, both of which he attributed to interest rate as "the villain of the piece".

It can be observed that the economic functioning will be in complete contrast if the same is driven by rate of returns to the real sector. The one-to-one mapping of both the real and financial sectors would increase investments, consumption, employment, and hence economic growth in direct proportion with the increase in the returns to the real sector. As a result, credit growth is tied closely to the expected growth rate of the real economy (Shaukat 2014). Accordingly, a risk-sharing-/equity-based Islamic system would not be expected to experience deep boom and busts cycles. Moderate and brief booms and recession may be generated by good crops, productivity, technical change, or adverse shocks. They cannot be generated by the financial system itself. Equilibrium in an Islamic economy thus structured will be stable, and the rate of return to the financial sector will be fully aligned with the profit rate in the real sector of the economy.

A number of influential scholars, in the past, proposed reforms that would abolish the credit system and replace it by an equity-based investment system. For instance, Walker (1873), Carroll (1965), Simons (1948), Friedman (1969), and Rothbard (1994) opposed fictitious credit creation by banks and favored the creation of joint-stock companies which use savings to buy equities. Among the most celebrated proposals along these lines was the plan formulated in the University of Chicago, "Chicago Memorandum" in 1933, which called for 100% reserve money and for an equity-based investment system. Irving Fisher (1933) claimed the following advantages for this plan: (i) much better control of a major source of business cycle fluctuations and sudden increases and contractions of bank credit and of the supply of bank-created money; (ii) complete elimination of bank runs; (iii) dramatic reduction in the (net) public debt; and (iv) dramatic reduction in private debt, as money creation no longer requires simultaneous debt creation.

A recent IMF paper titled "the Chicago Plan Revisited" studied the claims made by Fisher and others in favor of the Chicago Plan by embedding a comprehensive and carefully calibrated model of the banking system in a DSGE model of the U.S. economy. Moreover, Kotlikoff (2010) also made a proposal on similar lines suggesting "Limited Purpose Banking". LBP would essentially transform all financial intermediaries with limited liability into mutual fund companies, with a single regulatory agency the "Federal Financial Authority" taking care of the regulatory and supervisory roles. LBP would maintain a close link between the real and the financial sectors where the former will drive the latter.

It is often claimed that risk sharing, or Islamic finance, increases risks in the economy. There appears to be a conceptual confusion in cognition of the justification for finance. If finance is conceived as intermediating and facilitating the link between demand for finance emanating from the real sector and the supply of finance, then there must be a close link between the real and finance sectors of the economy. In this case, risks are taken in the real sector. When it comes to financing, the modality can be risk sharing, risk transfer, or risk shifting. But the overall risk of the activity seeking financing does not increase. The exception is when finance is decoupled from real sector activities as it happened during the run-up to the recent crisis. For a number of years during the 1990s, observers, including Hans Tietmier, the then President of Bundesbank, warned in international fora that "financial decoupling" was increasing the risks in global finance [Menkoff and Tolksorf (2001)]. These warnings were not attended to and consequences followed Epstein, G. (2006).

Continuation of a debt-based financing regime will not necessarily allow the benefits of emerging multipolarity to accrue to the world economy. The new system can be more effective with a new regime of financing. Indications are that almost all emerging countries in Asia are actively considering risk sharing via Islamic finance as a possible alternative. Quite a few are leveraging the "first-mover" status of Malaysia in education, manpower training, and instrument innovation in Islamic finance to introduce their own brand of risk sharing method of financing. If these efforts succeed, the benefits of emerging multiple growth centers will be buttressed further with greater stability and resilience in the supporting financial transactions through enhanced risk sharing. Even now, risk sharing could be an effective alternative to the debt-based ways and means of helping European countries facing sovereign debt crises. For example, Eurozone could issue long-term securities with payoffs based on the GDP performance in these countries. Similarly, China could buy Italian GDP-based securities rather than the consideration reportedly being given to purchase of Italian debt. These types of risk sharing instruments have been proposed by analysts such as Shiller (2003), for some time now. Recently, Farmer suggested central banks' purchase of equity shares to stabilize the equity markets [Farmer (2010)]. Perhaps the present regime's uncertainty has created a valuable opportunity to seek alternatives to the debt-based finance regime.

Notes

1. The 'butterfly effect' was a phrase discovered in Edward Lorenz's talk for the 139th meeting of the American Association for the Advancement of Science in 1972, titled "*Does the flap of a butterfly wing in Brazil set off a tornado in Texas.*"
2. Louis Bachelier (1900), in his thesis, the theory of speculation, developed the notions of stochastic process characterizing financial variables. Two main stochastic processes have become known in finance: the random walk and the martingale processes. A more encompassing approach to uncertainty uses Levy processes that allow for both jumps and smooth motion.
3. The authors introduced a comprehensive new historical database for studying banking crises, inflation, currency crashes, and debasements—unsurprisingly, currency and inflation crisis go hand in hand. Default through inflation has been more prevalent since World War I, as fiat money became the norm and links to gold eroded. Median inflation rates before World War I were well below those of the more recent period: 0.5% for 1500–1799 and 0.7% for 1800–1913 versus about 5% for 1914–2009 (see Reinhart and Rogoff 2011).
4. For a detailed discussion—based on historical evidence—on how a debt default translates into increasing country risk and eventually rating downgrades see Reinhart et al. (2003).
5. Eurozone as a whole has an unemployment rate of 12%.
6. Russia's default following the revolution holds the record, lasting 69 years. Greece's default in 1826 shuts it out from international capital markets for 53 consecutive years, while Honduras's 1873 default had a comparable duration (see Reinhart and Rogoff 2011).
7. Mauldin and Tepper (2011) contend that "Clearly, we are looking at a watershed event in public spending in the United States, United

Kingdom, and Europe. Because of the Great Financial Crisis, the usual benefit of a sharp rebound in cyclical tax receipts will not happen. It will take much longer to achieve any economic growth that could fill the public coffers.

8. See, for example, Shaukat (2014), Shaukat and Othman (2015), Mirakhor and Shaukat (2015), Askari et al. (2012), and Mirakhor (2010, 2011a, b).
9. There is no credit creation out of thin air in Islamic finance. Under conventional fractional reserve banking, deposits at one bank can be instantaneously loaned out or used to purchase a financial asset and become reserves and a basis for a new loan at a second bank. The credit multiplier is determined by the reserve requirement and could be high. In case of securitization and overleverage, the credit multiplier is theoretically infinite, leading to violent asset and product price fluctuations.
10. It is also to note that since interest rates are an economy-wide variable and therefore systematic, their risk does not get diversified away like other *idiosyncratic* risks of a stock would. This would also translate into a higher portfolio beta (see Bacha and Mirakhor 2015).

References

Arcand, J-L., Enrico, B., & Panizza., U. (2012). Too Much Finance? IMF Working Paper 12/161. Washington, USA.

Arrow, K. J. (1971). *Essays on the theory or risk-bearing*. Chicago: Markam.

Askari, H., et al. (2010). *Stability of Islamic finance*. Singapore: Wiley.

Askari, H., Iqbal, Z., Krichene, N., & Mirakhor, A. (2012). *Risk sharing in finance: The Islamic finance alternative*. Wiley: Singapore.

Bacha O. I., & Mirakho, A.. (2015). *A Risk Sharing Banking Model*. Presented at Inaugural Annual Symposium on Islamic Economics and Finance. The World Bank & IDB Istanbul 7th & 8th September, 2015.

Bachelier, L. (1900). *The theory of speculation*. Paris: Gauthier-Villars.

BIS (2010). *The future of public debt: Prospects and implications* (Working Papers No. 300). By Stephen et al., Monetary and Economics Department.

Carroll, C. H. (1965). *Organization of debt into currency and other papers*. Princeton, NJ: D. Van Nostrand Company.

Chorafas, D. N. (1994). *Chaos theory in the financial markets: Applying fractals, fuzzy logic, genetic algorithms, swarm simulation & the Monte Carlo method to manage market choas and volatility*. Burr Ridge, IL: IRWIN Professional Publishing.

Erbas S. N., & Mirakhor, A. (2007). The Equity Premium Puzzle, Ambiguity Aversion and Institutional Quality, IMF Working Paper, n. 07/230, Washington (DC): International Monetary Fund.

Epstein, G. (2006). *Financialization and the world economy*. New York: Edward Elgar.

Farmer, R. (2010). *How the economy works: Confidence, crashes, and self-fulfilling prophecies*. New York: Oxford University Press.

Fisher, I. (1933). The debt-deflation theory of great depressions. *Econometrica, 1*(4), 337–357.

Friedman, M. (1969). The optimum quantity of money. In M. Friedman (Ed.), *The optimum quantity of money and other essays* (pp. 1–50). Chicago: Aldine.

Goodwin, B. (1994). *How the leopard changed its spots: The evolution of complexity*. New York: Touchstone.

Johnson, N. (2007). *Simply complexity: A clear guide to complexity theory*. Oxford: One World Oxford.

Kaminsky, G. L., & Reinhart C. (1999) The twin crises: The causes of banking and balance of payments problems. *American Economic Review 89*(3), 473–500.

Kim, S., Kim, S. H., & Wang, Y. (2005). Regional versus global risk sharing in East Asia. *Asian Economic Papers, 3*(3), 182–201.

Kotlikoff, L. J. (2010). *Jimmy Stewart is dead: Ending the world's ongoing financial plague with limited purpose banking*. New York: Wiley.

Krugman, P. (1996). *The self-organizing economy* (This book is also a delightful introduction to the application of complexity to economics). Oxford: Basil Blackwell.

Lee, J. W., & Shin, K. (2008). *Welfare Implication of International Financial Integration*. Asian Development working paper series on Regional Economic Integration No. 20.

Lorenz, E. N. (1963). Deterministic non-periodic flow. *Journal of the Atmospheric Sciences, 20,* 130–141.

Lorenz, E. N. (1993). *The essence of chaos*. Seattle, WA: University of Washington Press.

Mandelbrot, B. B., & Hudson, R. (2004). *The (Mis) behaviour of markets: A fractal view of risk, ruin & reward*. New York: Perseus Books Group.

Mauldin, J., & Tepper, J. (2011). *End game: The end of debt super cycle and how it changes every thing*. Hoboken, NJ: Wiley.

Meadows, D. H. (2000). *"Thinking in Systems" White River Junction*. Vermont: Chelsea Green Publishing.

Menkoff, L., & Tolksorf (2001). *Financial market drift: Decoupling of the financial market from the real economy?* Heidelberg: Springer.

Mirakhor, A. (2010). *Whither Islamic finance? Risk sharing in an age of crises*. Paper presented at the Inaugural Securities Commission Malaysia (SC)—Oxford Centre for Islamic Studies (OCIS) Roundtable. *Developing a Scientific Methodology on Shariah Governance for Positioning Islamic Finance Globally*. March 15, 2010

Mirakhor, A. (2011a). *Islamic Finance in the Multi polar World*. Presented at the Asian Institute Finance Distinguished Speaker Series, Kuala Lumpur, 13 September 2011.

Mirakhor A., (2011b). *Epistemological Foundation of Finance: Islamic and Conventional*. Keynote address presented at the Foundations of Islamic Finance Conference Series, Kuala Lumpur. March 8–10, 2011.

Mirakhor, A., & Hamid, I. S. (2009). *Islam and development*. New York: Global Scholarly Publications.

Mirakhor, A., Krichene, N., & Shaukat, M. (2012). Unsustainability of the interest rate-based debt financing. *ISRA International Journal of Islamic Finance, 4*(2).

Paulos J. A. (2003), *The New Financial Order: Risks in the 21st Century*. USA: Princeton University Press.

Peters, E. E. (1996). *Chaos and order in the capital markets: A new view of cycles, prices, and market volatility* (2nd ed.). Hoboken, NJ: Wiley.

Progogine, I. (1980). *From being to becoming*. San Fransisco: W. H. Freeman and Company.

Progogine, I. (1989). *Exploring complexity*. New York: W. H. Freeman and Company.

Progogine, I. (1997). *The end of certainty*. New York: The Free Press.

Ramsey, F. P. (1928). A mathematical theory of saving. *Economic Journal, 38*(152), 543–559.

Reinhart, C., Reinhart V., & Rogoff K. (2012). Public debt overhangs: Advanced-economy episodes since 1800. *Journal of Economic Perspectives, 51 26*(3), 69–86.

Reinhart, C., & Rogoff K. (2010). *This time is different: Eight centuries of financial folly*. Princeton: Princeton University Press.

Reinhart, C., & Rogoff K. (2011). *Growth in a time of debt* (NBER Working Paper No. 15639).

Reinhart, C., Rogoff, K., & Savastano, M. (2003). Debt intolerance. *Brookings Papers on Economic Activity 1*, 1–74.

Rogoff, K. (2011). *Global imbalances without tears* (Project syndicate, 2011-03-01).
Rothbard, M. N. (1994). *The case against the fed*. Auburn, AL: Ludwig von Mises Institute.
Schwarcz, S. L. (2009). Regulating complexity in financial markets. *Washington University Law Review, 87*(2).
Shaukat, M. (2014). Financing economic growth with stability from Islamic perspective. *Journal of Islamic Business and Management, 4*(2).
Shaukat, M., & Othman, A. S. (2015). Instability of interest based debt financing and the Islamic finance alternative. *IRTI-IDB Journal of Islamic Economics Studies, 23*(2), 29–84.
Sheng, A. (2009). *From Asian to global financial crisis*. Cambridge: Cambridge University Press.
Shiller, T. (2003). *The new financial order*. Princeton: Princeton University Press.
Simons, H. C. (1948). *Economic policy for a free society*. Chicago, IL: University of Chicago Press.
Taleb, N. N. (2010 [2007]). *The black swan: The impact of the highly improbable*. New York: Random House and Penguin.
Turing, A. M. (1952). The chemical basis of morphogenesis. *Philosophical Transactions of the Royal Society of London. Series B, Biological Sciences, 237*(641), 37–72.
van Wincoop, E. (1999). How big are potential welfare gains from international risk sharing? *Journal of International Economics, 47*, 109–235.
Von Bertalanffy, L. (1969). *General System Theory*. New York: George Braziller. Revised Edition.
Walker, A. (1873). *The science of wealth*. Philadelphia, PA: J. B. Lippincott & Co.
Wheatley, M. J. (1992). *Leadership and the New Science: Learning About Organization from an Orderly Universe*. San Francisco: Berrett-Koehler.
World Bank Global Development Horizon. (2011). Washington, DC; see also Lin J. Y., & Dailami, M. *Are we prepared for a multipolar world economy?* (Project Syndicate, Syndicate.webarchive).
Zambelli, S., & George, D. (2012). *Nonlinearity, Complexity and Randomness in Economics: Towards Algorithmic Foundations for Economics*. USA: Wiley-Blackwell.

Index

S.A.R. Rizvi and I. Saba (eds.), *Developments in Islamic Finance*, Palgrave CIBFR Studies in Islamic Finance, DOI 10.1007/978-3-319-59342-5

The manufacturer's authorised representative in the EU is Springer Nature Customer Service Centre GmbH, Europaplatz 3, 69115 Heidelberg, Germany. If you have any concerns regarding our products, please contact ProductSafety@springernature.com

Printed and bound by CPI Group (UK) Ltd, Croydon, CR0 4YY
25/09/2026
02222890-0001